Civil War Novels

LC √√

GARLAND REFERENCE LIBRARY
OF THE HUMANITIES
(VOL. 700)

CIVIL WAR NOVELS
An Annotated Bibliography

Albert J. Menendez

GARLAND PUBLISHING, INC. • NEW YORK & LONDON
1986

Library of Congress Cataloging-in-Publication Data

Menendez, Albert J.
Civil War Novels.

(Garland reference library of the humanities ;
vol. 700)
Includes indexes.
1. American fiction—Bibliography.   2. United
States—History—Civil War, 1861–1865—Literature and
the war—Bibliography.   3. War stories, American—
Bibliography.   4. Historical fiction, American—
Bibliography.   I. Title.   II. Series: Garland
reference library of the humanities ; v. 700.
Z1231.F4M46   1986   001.3 s   86-18379
   [PS374.C53]   [813'.08'358]
   ISBN 0-8240-9933-8 (alk. paper)

Cover design by Renata Gomes

Printed on acid-free, 250-year-life paper
Manufactured in the United States of America

For Shirley

CONTENTS

Introduction and Acknowledgments

In this, the 125th anniversary of the beginning of the War Between the States and the 50th anniversary of the publication of <u>Gone With the Wind</u>, it seemed an appropriate time to prepare this bibliographical guide to over 1,000 Civil War novels. (I am using the term Civil War rather than any alternatives because it seems to be the most universally recognized term.)

For years I have been conscious of the need for a reader's guide to Civil War novels. With the exception of Robert A. Lively's trailblazing <u>Fiction Fights the Civil War</u> (University of North Carolina Press, 1957), there has been no guidebook to this important genre.

We Americans have had a passionate and unending love affair with the Civil War. More novels have been written about this romantic, divisive era than about any other period in U.S. history.

Certain kinds of stories and events seem most popular: North-South romances; the daring experiences of the blockade runners; spies, scouts, and espionage; life on the homefront; and detailed examinations of famous battles. These themes pervade Civil War fiction.

There is hardly a battle, an event, a prominent person, or region that has not been explored by novelists during the past century and a quarter. (One notable exception: The role of Catholic sisters, those "angels of mercy" who performed extraordinary acts of courage and compassion in battlefields and hospitals, has been completely ignored.)

Even the most obscure events have been immor-
talized in fiction. Such happenings as the Battle
of the Crater, a massacre of Confederate prisoners
in a small Missouri town, skirmishes at Wilson
Creek and Sand Creek, and Confederate intrigue in
Portland, Oregon have all served as the setting for
full-length novels.

Practically every geographical locale has its
own novel. Bermuda (Bruce Lancaster's Bride of a
Thousand Cedars), Idaho (Grover Guluk's A Drum
Calls West), Nevada (James M. Cain's Past All
Dishonor) and Oregon (Ernest Haycox's The Long
Storm) are just a few examples of the regional
diversity in Civil War fiction.

Civil War novels have always been popular,
judging by output and sales, though certain decades
(the 1860s, the 1930s, and the early 1960s) lead in
output. But there has been no decline in recent
years. Rita Mae Brown's High Hearts, John Calvin
Batchelor's American Falls, Tom Wicker's Unto This
Hour, Thomas Keneally's Confederates and John
Jakes' North and South are just a few recent books
that have made the bestseller lists or have
received wide critical acclaim.

I think it is a fair observation to assert
that the quality of Civil War novels is greater
today than a century ago. Perhaps it is the
distance that time gives that helps to make today's
novels more credible.

For 50 to 75 years following the conflict,
propaganda for one side or the other superceded
narrative integrity. Too many authors concentrated
on justifying their side, rather than trying to
present a balanced account.

Another problem with the earlier novels was
that many were more factual than fictional.
Reading numerous volumes published from the 1860s
through the 1890s, I was struck by how many
appeared to be personal memoirs of the authors
rather than genuine fiction. I have included them

in this book because the Library of Congress classifies them as fiction. But I still have my doubts and so will most readers.

Some of America's greatest authors (William Faulkner, Caroline Gordon, Robert Penn Warren) tried their hand at Civil War fiction and some succeeded in fashioning classics. As far as quality is concerned, perhaps 60 or 70 of these Civil War novels would be included in any comprehensive list of the most enduring fiction ever produced in this country.

This volume includes novels of the Civil War period, the Reconstruction South and some prewar novels dealing with slavery and plantation life. I have also included a few novels which are multi-generational but which include some Civil War scenes, e.g., Eugenia Price's Margaret's Story.

I have also included more than 120 novels designed for younger readers. This considerable output reveals how popular the Civil War has been as a subject for writers of young adult and juvenile books. I have designated these books by listing them under "Younger Readers" in the Subject Index.

The Subject Index has been designed to help readers find the books they want. If a reader is interested, say, in novels set in Kentucky, he or she will find 44 titles cited. There are 5 novels about John Wilkes Booth and 31 where Abraham Lincoln appears as a character. There is also a Title Index.

I would be remiss if I did not extend my appreciation to Ms. Roberta Engelman and her helpful staff at the University of North Carolina's Rare Book Collection. This Chapel Hill-based library includes the Wilmer Collection of Civil War Novels, the single most impressive source for students of this subject. The Wilmer Collection also includes short stories, plays and poems, as well as related material.

My wife Shirley helped at every stage in the
research and production of this guide.   To her it
is gratefully dedicated.

Albert J. Menendez
Gaithersburg, Maryland
June 1986

Civil War Novels

1. Abrahams, Robert. Mr. Benjamin's Sword.
Philadelphia: Jewish Publication Society,
1948.

   Designed for young adults, this novel
concentrates on the exciting escape of
statesman Judah P. Benjamin from Union-held
territory as the Confederacy was collapsing.
It details his later years as a successful
lawyer in England.

2. Adams, Julia Davis. Remember and Forget.
New York: Dutton, 1932.

   A romance of two Southern girls in the
Shenandoah Valley who keep the home fires
burning while their lovers are off fighting
for Lee and Jackson.

3. Adams, William T. At the Front. Boston:
Lee & Shepard, 1897.

4. ———. Brave Old Salt. Boston: Lee &
Shepard, 1866.

5. ———. Brother Against Brother. Boston:
Lee & Shepard, 1894.

6. ———. Fighting for the Right. Boston:
Lee & Shepard, 1892.

7. ———. Fighting Joe. Boston: Lee &
Shepard, 1866.

8. ———. In the Saddle. Boston: Lee &
Shepard, 1895.

9. ———. A Lieutenant at Eighteen. Boston:
Lee & Shepard, 1896.

10. ———. On the Blockade. Boston: Lee &
Shepard, 1891.

11. ———. On the Staff. Boston: Lee &
Shepard, 1897.

12. ———. The Sailor Boy. Boston: Lee &
Shepard, 1883.

13. ———. The Soldier Boy. Boston: Lee & Shepard, 1863.

14. ———. Stand By the Union. Boston: Lee & Shepard, 1892.

15. ———. Taken By the Enemy. Boston: Lee & Shepard, 1889.

16. ———. An Undivided Union. Boston: Lee & Shepard, 1899.

17. ———. A Victorious Union. Boston: Lee & Shepard, 1894.

18. ———. Within the Enemy's Lines. Boston: Lee & Shepard, 1890.

19. ———. The Yankee Middy. Boston: Lee & Shepard, 1866.

20. ———. The Young Lieutenant. Boston: Lee & Shepard, 1865.

These eighteen novels by William Adams were designed for young boys in the North. They feature Dexter Lyon of Kentucky, who fights for a Union cavalry operating mostly in Kentucky and Tennessee.

21. Alcott, Louisa May. Work: A Story of Experience. Boston: Roberts, 1873.

This celebrated New England author extolled the noble virtues of the nursing profession, which really began during the Civil War.

22. Aldrich, Bess Streeter. Song of Years. New York: Appleton, 1939.

A tale of Iowa pioneers which continues through the Civil War days.

23. Alexander, Holmes. American Nabob. New York: Harper, 1939.

The hero of this mediocre novel is an entrepeneur in prewar Virginia and West Virginia.

24. Alger, Horatio, Jr. Frank's Campaign. Boston: Loring, 1864.

Farm boys fight for the Union at Fredericksburg.

25. Allee, Marjorie Hill. The Road to Carolina. Boston: Houghton Mifflin, 1932.

Some Indiana Quakers are trapped in North Carolina for the duration of the war.

26. Allen, Henry. Journey to Shiloh. New York: Random House, 1960.

Seven Confederate soldiers from Texas fight at Shiloh.

27. ————. One More River to Cross. New York: Random House, 1967.

A former slave from Arkansas seeks a better life in the West but fails to find it fully.

28. ————. Summer of the Gun. Philadelphia: Lippincott, 1978.

A band of Confederate cavalry deserters descend on a small Texas town and kidnap a mother and daughter. Her Texas Ranger son and a freed slave track them down.

29. Allen, Hervey. Action At Aquilla. New York: Farrar, 1938.

A romance with vivid battle scenes, the action is seen through the eyes of a man who hated war. The Nation called it "a good run-of-the-mill Civil War novel." The reading public loved it but reviewers were less kind.

30. Allen, James Lane. The Sword of Youth. New York: Century, 1915.

A seventeen-year-old Kentucky boy joins
the Confederate Army in 1863, following in
the footsteps of his father and four
brothers who had already died for the cause.
His lonely mother was bitter, believing that
she had sacrificed enough for what to her
was already a lost cause. During the war he
deserts to visit his gravely ill mother but
is pardoned by Robert E. Lee at Appomattox.
One reviewer called it "a sentimental
romance tinged with psychological subtlety."
Allen's biographer, William Bottorff, called
this "a novel of man's search for values and
of his pursuit of goals in the light of a
code finally arrived at."

31. Allen, Merritt Parmelee. Blow, Bugles,
    Blow. New York: Longmans, 1956.

    The Civil War comes alive in this fine
    young adult novel focusing on Sheridan's
    army.

32. ———. Johnny Reb. New York: Longmans,
    1952.

    A South Carolina orphan boy joins Wade
    Hampton's army.

33. ———. White Feather. New York:
    Longmans, 1944.

    A Kentucky mountain boy fights with
    Morgan's Raiders and redeems himself in the
    eyes of his stern grandfather, who had once
    given him a white feather as a symbol of
    cowardice.

34. Allen, Stanton P. A Boy Trooper With
    Sheridan. Boston: Lothrop, 1899.

    The adventures of a young Union soldier in
    Sheridan's army.

35. Allis, Marguerite. The Rising Storm. New
    York: Putnam, 1955.

    Two twins are separated. One is raised in
    Ohio, the other in Louisiana. They meet on

a battlefield years later. There is a good depiction of prewar Cincinnati, a haven for runaway slaves.

36. Alter, Robert Edmond. _The Day of the Arkansas_. New York: Putnam, 1965.

A seventeen-year-old boy aboard the _C.S.S. Arkansas_ as it plies its way to Vicksburg, dreams of capturing a notorious Union spy.

37. Altsheler, Joseph A. _Before the Dawn_. New York: Doubleday, 1904.

The fall of Richmond.

38. ————. _The Guns of Bull Run_. New York: Appleton, 1914.

This is the first in a series of eight books for young adults featuring Harry Kenton, a young West Point graduate from Kentucky who fights for the South. All of Altsheler's novels are detailed and heavy on battle scenes. (_Before the Dawn_, _In Circling Camps_, and _The Last Rebel_ are adult novels and are not part of the Kenton series.)

39. ————. _The Guns of Shiloh_. New York: Appleton, 1914.

40. ————. _In Circling Camps_. New York: Appleton, 1900.

41. ————. _The Last Rebel_. Philadelphia: Lippincott, 1905.

42. ————. _The Rock of Chickamauga_. New York: Appleton, 1915.

43. ————. _The Scouts of Stonewall_. New York: Appleton, 1914.

44. ————. _The Shades of the Wilderness_. New York: Appleton, 1916.

45. ————. _The Star of Gettysburg_. New York: Appleton, 1915.

46. ———. The Sword of Antietam. New York:
    Appleton, 1914.

47. ———. The Tree of Appomattox. New York:
    Appleton, 1916.

48. Andrews, Annulet. Melissa Starke. New
    York: Dutton, 1955.

    A tale of the Reconstruction days.

49. Anderson, Alston. All God's Children.
    Indianapolis: Bobbs, Merrill, 1965.

    An escaped slave fights for the Union.

50. Anderson, Betty Baxter. Powder Monkey.
    Greenwich, CT: New York Graphic Society,
    1962.

    A story about naval battles on and near
    the Mississippi River.

51. Andrews, Mary Raymond Shipman. The Perfect
    Tribute. New York: Scribner, 1906.

    A heart-warming novella published shortly
    before the centennial of Lincoln's birth, it
    was widely popular in both North and South.
    It depicts the accidental visit of the
    kindly President to a dying Confederate
    soldier's bedside in a Washington hospital.
    Full of sentimental coincidences, it ends
    with the soldier holding Lincoln's hand as
    he dies. The famous story of Lincoln's
    scribbling of the Gettysburg Address on the
    back of an envelope may have originated with
    this charming tale.

52. Andrews, Robert. Great Day in the Morning.
    New York: Coward, 1950.

    Based on a real incident called "The
    Georgia Conspiracy," this is the tale of a
    charismatic Southerner who tries to bring
    Colorado into the Confederacy.

53. Anonymous. Blue and Grey. New Orleans:
    Graham, 1885.

A pro-Southern romance covering the war and Reconstruction in Louisiana.

54. ————. Kate Morgan and Her Soldiers. Philadelphia: American Sunday School Union, 1862.

55. ————. The Lady Lieutenant. Philadelphia: Barclay, 1863.

A Kentucky woman disguises herself as a Union soldier to be near her lover.

56. ————. The Lost Dispatch. Galesburg, IL: Galesburg Printing Company, 1889.

57. ————. The Old Flag. Philadelphia: American Sunday School Union, 1864.

58. ————. The Princess of the Moon. Warrenton, VA: Privately printed, 1869.

Sub-titled "A Confederate Fairy Story," this is a fantasy about a Confederate soldier who returns to the ruins of his home and encounters celestial beings.

59. ————. Uncle Daniel's Story of Tom Anderson and Twenty Great Battles. New York: A.R. Hart, 1886.

60. ————. Walter Graham, Statesman. Lancaster, PA: Fulton, 1891.

61. Appel, John W. The Light of Parnell. Philadelphia: Heidelberg Press, 1916.

A saga of Pennsylvanians who defend the Union.

62. Appell, George Charles. The Man Who Shot Quantrill. New York: Doubleday, 1957.

A taut, suspenseful tale of the Union Army man who captured the notorious Confederate marauder.

63. Arnold, Edgar. The Young Refugees. Richmond: Hermitage Press, 1912.

Two lads from Virginia fight for their
homeland at New Hope Church and elsewhere.

64. Ashley, C.B. Luke Bennett's Hideout. New
     York: John W. Lovell, n.d.

     The Battle of Vicksburg and related
     incidents of 1863.

65. Ashley, Robert. The Stolen Train.
     Philadelphia: Winston, 1953.

     The story of Andrew's Raiders.

66. Auchincloss, Louis. Watchfires. Boston:
     Houghton Mifflin, 1982.

     New York during the war is the background
     for this tale of the troubled marriage of a
     brilliant lawyer.

67. [Austin, Jane G.] Dora Darling: The
     Daughter of the Regiment. Boston:
     Tilton, 1865.

     Insipid romance with carciature of
     Southern dialect.

68. Avery, Myrta A. The Rebel General's Loyal
     Bride. Springfield, MA: W.J. Holland,
     1873.

     A Virginia family is divided by the wife's
     decision to support the Union.

69. Babcock, Bernie. The Soul of Abe Lincoln.
     Philadelphia: Lippincott, 1923.

     A young, engaged Southern couple is
     divided by the war. He joins the Union but
     she is pro-Confederate. They lose touch as
     she nurses Southern soldiers. He is now in
     the Secret Service in Washington and has met
     Lincoln. She comes to the Northern Capital,
     meets Lincoln and admires him. Though
     Lincoln's death intervenes, the couple's
     story has a happy ending. This book received
     good reviews for accuracy and vivid writing.

70. Babcock, William Henry. Kent Fort Manor.
    Philadelphia: Henry T. Coates, 1903.

    Civilian life is trying in and around
    wartime Washington.

71. Bacheller, Irving Addison. Father Abraham.
    Indianapolis: Bobbs-Merrill, 1925.

    A young Yankee leaves his harsh stepfather
    to live with a Southern uncle. He remains
    pro-Union when war comes. A fair romantic
    adventure, it includes Lincoln as a
    sympathetic character.

72. Bacon, Eugenia J. Lyddy: A Tale of the Old
    South. New York: Continental, 1898.

    A sympathetic and romantic portrait of
    slavery, arguing that there was a bond of
    affection in many areas between slave and
    owner. The hero was "one of God's black
    angels."

73. Bailey, Matilde. Right or Wrong. New
    Orleans: Graham, 1912.

    A conventional story set in New Orleans.

74. Baker, William Mumford. Inside: A
    Chronicle of Secession. New York:
    Harper, 1866.

    A Southern Unionist's view of the trials
    and sufferings of a loyal minister.

75. Ballard, Willis T. Trials of Rage. New
    York: Doubleday, 1975.

    A Union Army captain tries to halt
    Confederates who instigate Indian rebellions
    in the West.

76. Banks, Charles Eugene and George Cram Cooke.
    In Hampton Roads. Chicago: Rand, McNally,
    1899.

Features the Monitor and the Merrimac and
the love story of Virginia Eggleston of
Waverley Plantation in Virginia.

77. Bannister, Don. Long Day at Shiloh. New
York: Knopf, 1981.

Details the first twenty-four hours of the
battle, beginning with the daily routine in
a Union camp.

78. Barbe, Muriel Culp. A Union Forever.
Glendale, CA: The Barbe Associates,
1949.

A fifteen-year-old orphan boy from
Illinois meets Abraham Lincoln and
eventually joins the Union army.

79. Barney, Helen Corse. Green Rose of Furley.
New York: Crown, 1953.

A Quaker girl's farm serves as a refuge
for escaped slaves.

80. Barrow, Frances Elizabeth. Colonel Freddy.
New York: Leavitt & Allen, 1863.

A portrait of the Zouaves.

81. ————. The Orphan's Home Mittens. New
York: Appleton, 1865.

The Battle of Roanoke Island.

82. Bartlett, Major W.C. An Idyl of War-Times.
New York: Vanderpoole, 1890.

A love story set in New York, Maryland and
Tennessee.

83. Bartlett, Napier. Clarimonde. Richmond:
Malsby, 1863.

Written during the war itself, this is a
romance set in New Orleans.

84. Barton, William E. A Hero In Homespun.
Boston: Lamson, Wolffe & Company, 1897.

A tale of eastern Kentuckians loyal to the Union. "Homespun hero of the Southern Appalachians has emerged from obscurity and turned the tide of battle."

85. ————. Pine Knot. New York: Appleton, 1900.

A daughter of an abolitionist teacher marries a Confederate officer from Kentucky rather than a chaplain in the Union Army.

86. Basso, Hamilton. The Light Infantry Ball. New York: Doubleday, 1959.

Southern plantation society rapidly disintegrates. The hero is a Northern-educated planter's son who is reluctantly drawn into the war. Christian Century said this story of life on the homefront had the "scent of mimosa and fading roses."

87. Batchelor, John Calvin. American Falls. New York: Norton, 1985.

A highly praised novel concentrating on espionage.

88. Baylor, Frances Courtenay. Behind the Blue Ridge. Philadelphia: Lippincott, 1887.

The lives of the mountain people of Virginia.

89. Beard, Oliver Thomas. Bristling With Thorns. Detroit: Detroit News Company, 1884.

A Mississippi man is enthusiastic about the Confederate nation in this saga covering many years and battles.

90. Beatty, John. McLean. Columbus, OH: Fred J. Heer, 1904.

An Ohio infantryman is captured but escapes from a Rebel P.O.W. camp.

91. Beatty, Patricia. Blue Stars Watching. New York: Morrow, 1969.

   A brother and sister are sent to their aunt in San Francisco to escape the dangers of the war in Delaware. In California they become involved in even greater peril in this story about a Confederate conspiracy and the beginning of the Union Secret Service.

92. ————. I Want My Sunday, Stranger! New York: Morrow, 1977.

   In 1863 the horse (Sunday) of a Mormon boy from California is stolen by Confederate soldiers. The boy runs away, determined to recover his lightening-fast companion, and encounters the human suffering of the war from Texas to Arkansas to Gettysburg. Well written and well researched.

93. Bechdolt, Frederick Ritchie. Bold Raiders of the West. New York: Doubleday, 1940.

   Cavalry action in New Mexico.

94. Becker, Stephen D. When the War Is Over. New York: Random House, 1969.

   A Kentucky orphan boy becomes a Rebel guerilla and wounds a Union officer sixteen days after Appomattox. The officer survives and befriends him, but the boy is executed during the hysteria following Lincoln's death.

95. Beebe, Elswyth Thane. Yankee Stranger. New York: Duell, 1944.

   A romantic account of civilian life behind the front in Virginia.

96. Beecher, Henry Ward. Norwood. New York: Scribner, 1868.

   The prominent Yankee preacher defends the virtues of his beloved North.

97. Beffel, Eulalie. The Hero of Antietam. New
    York: Dutton, 1943.

    A somewhat farcical account of two
    generals who find themselves living side by
    side in a small Illinois town after the war.
    They are rivals in several amorous
    adventures. An uneven novel that showed
    some promise.

98. Bellah, James Warner. The Valiant
    Virginians. New York: Ballantine, 1953.

    General Jubal Early fights in the
    Shenandoah.

99. Benadum, Clarence Edward. Bates House. New
    York: Greenberg, 1951.

    A young Southern girl loves a Yankee
    lawyer in this exciting yarn noted for
    realistic salty dialogue and many battle
    scenes.

100. Benner, Judith A. Lone Star Rebel. Winston
    Salem: John F. Blair, 1971.

    A Texas boy becomes a courier to the
    Confederate cavalry.

101. Bennett, John Henry. So Shall They Reap.
    New York: Doubleday, 1944.

    Two poor white families continue an old
    feud throughout the war. This book shows
    the attitude of poor whites who wore the
    grey but despised the aristocrats who
    dominated Southern life. This tough,
    violent, action-filled narrative also shows
    desertion in the Confederate Army.

102. Benson, Blackwood Ketcham. Bayard's Courier.
    New York: Macmillan, 1902.

    Adventures of a Union cavalryman in the
    war's first year.

103. ———. A Friend With the Countersign. New
    York: Macmillan, 1901.

Love and espionage after the Battle of Gettysburg.

104. ———. Old Squire. New York: Macmillan, 1903.

A black man plays an important role at Gettysburg.

105. ———. Who Goes There? New York: Macmillan, 1900

A Union spy with amnesia is drafted into the Confederate Army.

106. Bentley, Robert T. Forestfield. New York: Grafton Press, 1903.

Saga of a plantation in the Old South and how war destroyed a way of life.

107. Bill, A.H. The Beleaguered City. New York: Knopf, 1946.

What Richmond was like during the four years it was the Confederate capital.

108. Bingham, Frazier Franklin. Ashore at Maiden's Walk. New York: Broadway, 1913.

A Florida man and his daughter, trying to get a load of cotton through the blockade, are captured by a Federal gunboat.

Blake, William. See Blech, William James.

109. Blech, William James. The Copperheads. New York: Dial Press, 1941.

In New York City a German immigrant's daughter is loved by three men, including a Union soldier and a Copperhead. The atmosphere of New York is impressively recreated, particularly the Draft Riots of 1863. Clifton Fadiman called this "a sort of Jacobinical secret history of the Civil War cast in the most outlandish fictional form."

110. Bodder, Charles H. <u>Under Fire with</u>
     <u>Farragut</u>. New York: Signal Boy
     Publications, 1919.

     Life on the <u>U.S.S. Richmond</u> as seen
     through the eyes of a sailor boy.

111. Bogue, Herbert Edwards. <u>Dareford</u>. Boston:
     C.M. Clark, 1907.

     A Vermont man fights at Gettysburg and in
     the Shenandoah.

112. Borland, Hal. <u>The Amulet</u>. Philadelphia:
     Lippincott, 1957.

     A Colorado orphan boy fights for the
     Confederacy in Missouri. His exploits and
     adventures are told in the form of exciting
     vignettes.

113. Bosher, Mrs. Kate Lee Langley. <u>Bobbie</u>.
     Richmond: B.F. Johnson, 1899.

     A young man goes to war leaving his
     sweetheart with a promise that he will
     return at Christmas to marry her.

114. Bowles, Colonel John. <u>The Stormy Petrel</u>.
     New York: Lovell, 1892.

     A saga of the Border States.

115. Bowley, F.S. <u>A Boy Lieutenant</u>.
     Philadelphia: Henry Altemus, 1906.

     A first person narrative of a white man
     from Massachusetts who heads a regiment of
     black troops who fight in Virginia.

116. Boyd, James. <u>Marching On</u>. New York:
     Scribner, 1927.

     A poor farmer's son loves the daughter of
     a wealthy planter but the war comes before
     they can marry. He fights, spends two years
     in prison and returns to the girl he loves
     in the beaten Southland. <u>Literary Review</u>
     said the author "has done for the Southern

soldier what Stephen Crane did for the
Northern soldier and he has done it somewhat
better." The New York Times called it "a
very fine and memorable novel."

117.   Boyd, Thomas Alexander. Samuel Drummond.
       New York: Scribner, 1925.

       An Ohio farm couple face hard times when
       war comes. The husband enlists and the farm
       decays. Afterwards, it takes incredible
       endurance to build back a semblance of
       prosperity. Valuable for a depiction of the
       social and economic forces which accompanied
       wartime.

118.   Boyle, Virginia Frazier. Brokenburne. New
       York: E.R. Herrick, 1897.

       Written in dialect this is a happy view of
       Southern plantation life.

119.   Boyles, Kate and Virgil D. The Hoosier
       Volunteer. Chicago: McClurg, 1914.

       The friendship of two schoolboys continues
       through the battle of Vicksburg.

       Boylston, Peter. See Curtis, George
       Ticknor.

120.   Bradbury, Bianca. Flight Into Spring. New
       York: Washburn, 1965.

       A Maryland girl marries a grim puritanical
       farmer and goes to live with his parents on
       a rugged farm in Connecticut. Even though
       her family were Northern sympathizers, her
       Yankee in-laws consider her a Southerner and
       dislike her intensely.

121.   Bradford, Roark. Kingdom Coming. New York:
       Harper, 1933.

       A black boy is left in charge of a
       Louisiana plantation where he becomes
       restless. A vivid picture of black life.

122. ———. Three Headed Angel. New York:
Harper, 1937.

The saga of a Tennessee family that
acquired wealth and lived to enjoy it.

123. Brady, Cyrus Townsend. As the Sparks Fly
Upward. Chicago: McClurg, 1911.

A torrid romance.

124. ———. The Last Hope. New York: Dodd,
Mead, 1906.

125. ———. A Little Traitor to the South. New
York: Macmillan, 1904.

A wartime comedy with a tragic interlude
about the torpedoing of the Housatonic.

126. ———. On the Old Kearsage. New York:
Scribner, 1909.

Two seventeen-year-olds encounter one
another several times during the war. On
opposite sides, they eventually meet when a
Union ship sinks a Confederate one.

127. ———. The Patriots. New York: Dodd,
Mead, 1906.

A tangled romance with General Lee as the
hero.

128. ———. Secret Service. New York: Dodd,
Mead, 1912.

The novelized version of William
Gillette's spy tale about a Southern girl
who sacrifices all for love and a Northern
boy who sacrifices all for honor. The
entire story takes place in one night in
Richmond in the Spring of 1865.

129. ———. The Southerners. New York:
Scribner, 1903.

An officer in the Navy returns to Alabama
just after Lincoln's election. He chooses
to stay with the Union when war breaks out.

130. ————. Three Daughters of the Confederacy. New York: Dillingham, 1904.

    Three strong Southern women, two of who love Yankees, survive the war. Brady, an Episcopalian rector, once wrote: "Of all the novels and romances I have written, those of the Civil War have met with the warmest welcome and have elicited the highest praise." He also wrote a collection of short stories about the war called Woven with Ships.

131. Branch, Houston, and Frank Waters. Diamond Head. New York: Farrar, 1948.

    This recounts the exploits of the Confederate cruiser Shenandoah, which was sent into the Northern Pacific to hunt down the New England whaling fleet. Romantic but with mixed reviews.

132. Brandewine, Rebecca. The Outlaw Hearts. New York: Warner, 1986.

    A schoolteacher, emotionally ravaged by the Civil War, moves to a small town in the Ozark Mountains. Strangely enough, she falls in love with the notorious raider Luke Morgan. Publishers Weekly called it "a tale filled with the lore of the Ozarks and marked by good historical research and well-drawn characters."

133. Branscom, Alexander C. Mystic Romances of the Blue and the Gray. New York: Mutual, 1883.

    A series of unconnected events that barely constitutes a novel.

134. Branson, H.C. Salisbury Plain. New York: Dutton, 1965.

    A young captain narrates the story of the disintegration of a Union Army division in Virginia as a result of internal friction.

135. Brautigan, Richard. <u>A Confederate General</u>
      <u>from Big Sur</u>. New York: Grove Press,
      1965.

      This first novel is an absurd fantasy in
      which one character claims to be descended
      from a Confederate general. It contains a
      few italicized flashbacks to the Civil War,
      which the author calls "the last good time
      this country ever had."

136. Breslin, Howard. <u>A Hundred Hills</u>. New
      York: Crowell, 1960.

137. Brick, John. <u>Jubilee</u>. New York:
      Doubleday, 1956.

      In 1862 a young West Pointer joins a New
      York volunteer infantry and serves with
      valor under Sherman. <u>The Christian Science</u>
      <u>Monitor</u> called it "well written, absorbing,
      fast-paced."

138. ————. <u>The Richmond Raid</u>. New York:
      Doubleday, 1963.

      Colonel Dahlgren's cavalry unsuccessfully
      tries to liberate Union prisoners of war in
      Richmond.

139. ————. <u>Troubled Spring</u>. New York:
      Farrar, 1950.

      Sam, a soldier, is released from
      Andersonville and returns home to a little
      Hudson River town, where he discovers that
      his brother has married his girlfriend after
      Sam had been reported killed. His beloved
      town has changed; war profiteering and greed
      dominate. The hero finds his town will
      never be the same again and decides to
      leave.

140. ————. <u>Yankees on the Run</u>. New York:
      Duell, 1961.

      Two Union soldiers escape from Anderson-
      ville and try to make it to safety.

141. Brier, Royce. Boy in Blue. New York:
     Appleton, 1937.

     Emphasizes the ordinary Union private's
     life during the Battle of Chickamauga. A
     strong military emphasis.

142. Bristow, Gwen. The Handsome Road. New
     York: Crowell, 1938.

     A rich family and a very poor one cope
     with the Civil War and Reconstruction in a
     Louisiana river town. Filled with colorful
     incidents and adventures, this novel's
     depiction of a poor white girl's point of
     view is almost unique.

143. Bromfield, Louis. Wild Is the River. New
     York: Harper, 1941.

     Conflict breaks out between Union soldiers
     and proud Creoles in occupied New Orleans.
     Two ways of life are in conflict. Heavy
     into sex and romance, Bromfield shows the
     contrasts between the repressed Puritans
     from New England and sensuous Southerners.

144. Bronson, Lynn. The Runaway. Philadelphia:
     Lippincott, 1953.

     A young man serves General Grant.

     Brown, Caroline. See Krout, Caroline
     Virginia.

145. Brown, Katherine Holland. The Father. New
     York: Day, 1928.

     An abolitionist editor in Illinois
     attracts Abraham Lincoln with his editorials
     and they become friends just before
     Lincoln's election.

146. Brown, Karl. The Cup of Trembling. New
     York: Duell, Sloan, and Pearce, 1853.

     Harriet Beecher Stowe's son Frederick, a
     captain in the Union Army, is gravely
     wounded at Gettysburg.

147. Brown, Rita Mae. <u>High Hearts</u>. New York: Bantam, 1986.

A young woman, a tomboy Scarlett O'Hara, disguises herself as a man so she can follow her newly wed husband into the Confederate Army.

148. Browne, George Waldo. <u>A Daughter of Maryland</u>. New York: Novelist Publishing Company, 1895.

Pickett's last charge at Gettysburg.

149. Browne, Junius Henri. <u>Four Years in Secessia</u>. Hartford: O.D. Case, 1865.

The perilous journey of a war correspondent, including his many escapes from prison.

150. Browne, Walter Scott. <u>Andrew Bentley</u>. Camden, NJ: A.C. Graw, 1900.

A man from a village in western Pennsylvania retrieves his honor and becomes a hero. In a tearful ending he marries his beloved on his deathbed.

151. Bruce, Jerome. <u>Studies in Black and White</u>. New York: Neale, 1906.

A poorly written pro-slavery novel set on the Carolina coast.

152. Bryan, Mary E. <u>Wild Work: The Story of the Red River Tragedy</u>. New York: Appleton, 1881.

The carpetbagger era.

153. Bryce, Clarence Archibald. <u>Kitty Dixon; a Wee Bit of Love and War</u>. Richmond: Southern Clinic Press, 1907.

A Yankee girl in Old Virginia gives her heart to a Southern boy.

154. Buck, Charles W. Colonel Bob and a Double
     Love. Louisville: Standard Press, 1922.

     Southerners in Georgia and Kentucky
     struggle to survive the war.

155. Buck, Irving A. Cleburne and His Command.
     New York: Neale, 1909.

     A Confederate soldier reminisces about the
     Battle of Shiloh.

156. Buckley, Richard Wallace. The Last of the
     Houghtons. New York: Neale, 1907.

     A family is torn asunder because of
     conflicting loyalties about the war.

     Buckmaster, Henrietta. See Henkle,
        Henrietta.

157. Burchard, Peter. Jed. New York: Coward,
     1960.

     A novella of a young Union soldier who
     befriends a Mississippi farm boy and his
     family after Shiloh. When fellow Yankees
     try to pillage the farm, Jed stops them in a
     courageous act. Commonweal found it
     "memorable and deeply moving."

158. ———. North by Night. New York: Coward,
     1962.

     Two Union soldiers escape from a Rebel
     prison camp in search of Yankee lines.

159. ———. Rat Hall. New York: Coward, 1971.

     Dozens of Yankee prisoners escape from
     Libby Prison in Richmond in 1864.

160. Burchell, Sidney Herbert. The Shepherd of
     the People. London: Gay & Hancock,
     1924.

     Lincoln appears in a sympathetic role in a
     domestic novel which concentrates on social
     life in Civil War Washington.

161. Burnett, William Riley. The Dark Command: A Kansas Iliad. New York: Knopf, 1938.

A woman loves two men in the Kansas-Missouri border area during the early years of the war. Burnett shows the violent political differences in raw, frontier-like communities.

162. ————. The Goodhues of Sinking Creek. New York: Harper, 1934.

Political hatreds and personal feuds. The hero opposes secession and abolition.

163. Burow, Daniel R. Sound of the Bugle. St. Louis: Concordia, 1973.

A German immigrant in Georgia experiences the horrors of Sherman's March.

164. Burress, John. Bugle In the Wilderness. New York: Vanguard, 1958.

Life on the homefront in a small Missouri town seen through the eyes of a twelve-year-old boy. Burress shows how families and communities were riven by war divisions.

165. Bushnell, Belle. John Arrowsmith, Planter. Cedar Rapids, IA: Torch Press, 1910.

Louisiana plantation life.

166. Buster, Greene B. Brighter Sun. New York: Pageant, 1954.

Slaves use the Underground Railroad to escape a Kentucky plantation.

167. Cable, George Washington. The Cavalier. New York: Scribner, 1901.

Cavalry action in Mississippi.

168. ————. Dr. Sevier. Boston: Osgood, 1885.

The Reconstruction brings many unwanted changes to Louisiana Creoles.

169. ————. John March, Southerner. New York: Scribner, 1894.

A controversial novel which made Cable so unpopular that he left his native Louisiana for Massachusetts. Set in Reconstruction days, it concludes that the Union cause was essentially just.

170. ————. Kincaid's Battery. New York: Scribner, 1908.

A drawing-room romance set in New Orleans in the early days of the war.

171. Cain, James M. Mignon. New York: Dial, 1962.

A beautiful young widow and her father come to New Orleans at the close of the war, hoping to improve their fortunes. Cotton smuggling lands the father in jail, while irresistible Mignon links up with a discharged Union soldier. "Blood and lust," commented The New York Times.

172. ————. Past All Dishonor. New York: Knopf, 1946.

In Virginia City, Nevada a handsome Confederate spy falls in love with a hooker. Library Journal called it "a violent and explosive story written with gusto and skill," but The New York Times called it "a horse opera," and Edmund Wilson said this was "Cain at his nadir."

Cairns, Kate. See Bosher, Mrs. Kate Lee Langley.

173. Caldwell, James F. The Stranger. New York: Neale, 1907.

A romance between a Northern school-teacher and a Southern man in the Reconstruction South.

174. Calhoun, Alfred Rochefort. <u>Reunited</u>. New
     York: Bonner, 1890.

     A widow's two sons fight on opposite sides
     in Tennessee and Kentucky.

175. Campbell, Marie. <u>A House With Stairs</u>. New
     York: Rinehart, 1950.

     A white girl and a black girl, who is the
     narrator, grow up together on a Southern
     plantation during the war and Reconstruc-
     tion. This charming, sentimental novel
     presents a favorable view of Southern race
     relations.

176. Campbell, Thomas B. <u>Old Miss</u>. Boston:
     Houghton Mifflin, 1929.

     A charming, memorable, but rather dull
     story about the rise and fall of a Virginia
     woman.

177. Carr, Clark E. <u>The Illini</u>. Chicago:
     McClurg, 1904.

     An Illinois saga including some incidents
     in the Underground Railway.

178. Carr, John Dickson. <u>Papa La Bas</u>. New York:
     Harper, 1968.

     In 1858 New Orleans, future Confederate
     statesman, Judah P. Benjamin, solves a
     mystery.

179. Carrighar, Sally. <u>The Glass Dove</u>. New
     York: Doubleday, 1962.

     An Ohio farm becomes a stop on the
     Underground Railroad. The father joins the
     Union Army and his daughter manages the
     farm. She tends a wounded soldier and falls
     in love with him though he is suspected of
     being a spy.

180. Carroll, Curt. <u>The Golden Herd</u>. New York:
     Morrow, 1950.

The romance of a German immigrant's son in
Texas. The war brought hard times and the
cotton planters had to convert their
plantations to cattle ranches. Vivid and
colorful.

181. Carter, Forrest. Gone to Texas. New York:
Delacorte, 1975.

An adventure tale of Reconstruction days
in Missouri and Texas.

Castlemon, H.C. See Fosdick, Charles.

182. Castor, Henry. The Spanglers. New York:
Doubleday, 1948.

Andersonville prison horrors.

183. Catton, Bruce. Banners at Shenandoah. New
York: Doubleday, 1955.

The dean of Civil War historians concentrates on General Sheridan's cavalry in a
novel aimed at young readers.

184. Cavanah, Frances. A Patriot in Hoops. New
York: McBride, 1932.

A twelve-year-old Maryland girl attends
Lincoln's inauguration and falls in love
with the Union cause for which her father
also fights. She carries an important
message to the President later in the story.

185. Chambers, Robert William. Ailsa Paige. New
York: Appleton, 1910.

A picture of New York just before and
after Fort Sumter is fired upon.
Enthusiastic volunteers leave for the front
and are soon jolted by the horrible reality
of war. Chambers was a widely popular
writer of society novels before turning to
the Civil War.

186. ———. The Haunts of Men. New York:
Bacheller, 1898.

His poorest novel, a series of loosely connected incidents.

187. ———. Secret Service Operator 13. New York: Appleton, 1934.

A lively and entertaining espionage novel, the author's forte.

188. ———. Special Messenger. New York: Appleton, 1909.

A stirring portrait of a female spy.

189. ———. Whistling Cat. New York: Appleton, 1932.

Two young Texans serve the Union Army as telegraph operators. Most reviewers found it pedantic and melodramatic.

190. Channing, Justin. Southern Blood. New York: Bantam, 1980.

A prominent Southern family loses all in the war and, forsaking the U.S., vows to build a new life in England.

191. Chapin, Mrs. Sallie F. Fitz-Hugh St. Clair, the South Carolina Rebel Boy. Charleston, SC: Greer, 1872.

A pro-Southern romance.

192. Chaplin, Jane Dunbar. Out of the Wilderness. Boston: Henry A. Young, 1870.

A black saga.

193. Cheney, Brainard. Lightwood. Boston: Houghton Mifflin, 1939.

In Reconstruction Georgia farmers struggle against a Yankee-owned corporation bent on taking their land. An uneven novel of class struggle, about which The New York Times said, "It just misses being a first-rate job."

194. Cheney, Cora. <u>Fortune Hill</u>. New York: Holt, 1950.

A young adult novel about the search for buried gold in North Florida during the war.

195. Child, Lydia. <u>A Romance of the Republic</u>. Boston: Ticknor & Fields, 1867.

A sentimental love story of the Louisiana quadroons written by an abolitionist author.

196. Chittenden, L.E. <u>An Unknown Heroine</u>. New York: George H. Richmond, 1894.

A near-dead Vermont soldier is nursed by a Virginia woman whose husband is a Confederate prisoner of war. Because she helped the Yankee escape, he helps secure her husband's release.

197. Churchill, Winston. <u>The Crisis</u>. New York: Macmillan, 1901.

A classic study of the motivation, power and drama of war and its warriors.

Churton, Henry. See Tourgee, Albion.

Clark, Henry Scott. See Cox, Millard F.

Clarke, Covington. See Venable, Clarke.

198. Clarkson, Charles Ervine. <u>A Rose of Old Virginia</u>. Fort Smith, AK: Calvary-McBride, 1927.

A romantic novella.

199. Clay, Josephine Russell. <u>Frank Logan</u>. New York: Abbey, 1901.

A dancer becomes a Northern hero during the war and a U.S. Senator from Kentucky afterwards.

200. Clemens, Jeremiah. _Tobias Wilson_.
     Philadelphia: Lippincott, 1865.

     A sympathetic portrait of Union supporters
     in northern Alabama, written by a one-time
     U.S. Senator who dissented from the
     Confederate cause.

201. Coatsworth, Elizabeth. _George and Red_. New
     York: Macmillan, 1946.

     Two boys live near Niagara Falls and are
     friends though their fathers take sharply
     different positions on the war.

202. Cobb, Irvin S. _Red Likker_. New York:
     Cosmopolitan, 1929.

     More about the Kentucky liquor industry
     than the Civil War.

203. Cochran, Hamilton. _The Dram Tree_.
     Indianapolis: Bobbs-Merrill, 1961.

     A romantic novel of the blockade runners,
     which includes a legend of a dram tree.

204. Cochran, John S. _Bonnie Belmont_. Wheeling:
     Wheeling News Co., 1907.

     A romance of the war set in Ohio.

205. Cochran, Katherine. _Posie_. Cincinnati:
     Robert Clarke, 1896.

     Posie is the wife of a Union Army captain
     stationed in St. Augustine, Florida after
     the war. The Reconstruction changes the
     town's traditional Spanish character.

206. Coffin, Charles Carleton. _Winning His Way_.
     Boston: Ticknor & Fields, 1865.

     Ohio farmers respond to the Union call.

207. Coker, Elizabeth Boatwright. _Blood Red
     Roses_. New York: Dutton, 1977.

     Angelica, a beautiful Virginian, marries a
     cotton planter and moves to Hilton Head,

South Carolina on the eve of secession. The family lawyer, a Yankee spy, falls in love with her. Union soldiers occupy Port Royal, and Angelica is trapped behind enemy lines. The title is from a sea chantey.

208.   ————. The Day of the Peacock. New York: Dutton, 1952.

A colonel returns to the farmland of South Carolina to find his plantation in ruins and his status diminished. He concentrates on rebuilding his way of life.

209.   ————. India Allan. New York: Dutton, 1953.

A colorful narrative of South Carolina life from 1850 to 1876.

210.   ————. La Belle. New York: Dutton, 1959.

A beautiful mother and daughter team become camp followers to Sherman's troops.

211.   Coleman, Lonnie. Look Away, Beulah Land. New York: Doubleday, 1977.

The residents of a Georgia plantation try to create a new life as they experience the passing of the old ways.

Collingwood, Harry. See Lancaster, William Joseph.

212.   Collingwood, Herbert W. Andersonville Violets. Boston: Lee & Shepard, 1889.

Misery at the South Georgia prison.

213.   Collins, C.B. Tom and Joe. Richmond: Everett Waddey, 1890.

Two Louisiana farm boys fight for the grey. Set mostly in New Orleans around the Christmas of 1864.

214.   Colton, Arthur. Bennie Ben Cree. New York: Doubleday, 1900.

A Northern gunboat goes South in 1862.

215. Colver, Ann. <u>Mr. Lincoln's Wife</u>. New York: Farrar, 1943.

A sympathetic biographical novel which depicts Mrs. Lincoln as a strong figure.

216. Conrad, Thomas N. <u>A Confederate Spy</u>. New York: J.S. Ogilvie, n.d.

Purported reminiscences of a scout for Jeb Stuart.

217. Cooke, John Esten. <u>Hammer and Rapier</u>. New York: G.W. Carlton, 1870.

A retelling of the Virginia campaigns.

218. ————. <u>Hilt to Hilt</u>. New York: G.W. Carleton, 1869.

Cavalry action in western Virginia in 1864.

219. ————. <u>Mohun</u>. New York: F.J. Huntington, 1869.

Richmond's last days as the Confederate capital are seen through the eyes of a sympathetic observer. All of Cooke's novels were justifiably popular because of their strong characters and vivid dialogue.

220. ————. <u>Surry of Eagles Nest</u>. New York: Bunce & Huntington, 1866.

Focuses on Jackson and Stuart and their military strategy.

221. Corbett, Elizabeth F. <u>Faye's Folly</u>. New York: Appleton, 1941.

A farmer's daughter is in love with a married Union soldier in this romance set in Illinois. <u>Saturday Review</u> called it "a quiet little story of love and charm." <u>The New York Times</u> thought it was "readable and

entertaining" and had a "stirring war
setting."

222. Corrington, John William. *And Wait for the
Night*. New York: Putnam, 1964.

A pro-Southern view of the war and Union
occupation of Shreveport. *Library Journal*
thought it was "powerful and well-written"
but several reviewers thought it an exercise
in nostalgia.

223. Cotes, Joseph Hornor. *The Counterpart*. New
York: Macaulay, 1909.

A Northern soldier is tricked by a
Southern girl into revealing information
which leads to a disaster. *The New York
Times* said it was "written with unusual care
and considerable skill."

224. Coulson, George James Atkinson. *The Clifton
Picture*. Philadelphia: Lippincott,
1878.

Blockade running in Charleston.

225. Cox, Millard F. *The Legionnaires*.
Indianapolis: Bowen-Merrill, 1899.

A West Point graduate in southern Indiana
casts his lot with the Confederacy, but
marries a Union girl after the war.

226. Crabb, Alfred Leland. *Breakfast at the
Hermitage*. Indianapolis: Bobbs Merrill,
1945.

Crabb wrote seven novels about the war and
Reconstruction in Tennessee, about which *The
New York Times* commented, "These Nashville
stories of Dr. Crabb are pleasant but minor
accomplishments." In *Breakfast* a poor boy
becomes an architect in postwar Nashville.

227. ———. *Dinner at Belmont*. Indianapolis:
Bobbs-Merrill, 1942.

Vignettes of a captured city.

228. ————. Home To Tennessee. Indianapolis:
Bobbs-Merrill, 1952.

A grim tale of fratricidal warfare.

229. ————. Lodging at the Saint Cloud.
Indianapolis: Bobbs-Merrill, 1946.

Mostly about Confederate spies, including
appearances by General Nathan Forrest and
the widow of President Polk.

230. ————. A Mocking Bird Sang at Chickamauga.
Indianapolis: Bobbs Merrill, 1949.

A rather old-fashioned moral tale, filled
with daredevil adventures, about General
Forrest's exploits around Chattanooga in the
summer of 1863.

231. ————. Peace At Bowling Green.
Indianapolis: Bobbs-Merrill, 1955.

The only Crabb novel to concentrate on
Kentucky's role in the Civil War.

232. ————. Reunion at Chattanooga.
Indianapolis: Bobbs Merrill, 1950.

A daughty grandmother and her two sons
adjust to a changing life after the war
though its memories never fade.

233. ————. Supper at the Maxwell House.
Indianapolis: Bobbs Merrill, 1943.

A new restaurant opens in Nashville in
1869, symbolizing better days ahead. Rich
in historical detail, this novel includes an
appearance by President Andrew Johnson.

Craddock, Charles Egbert. See Murfree,
Mary.

234. Craig, Mrs. Benjamin H. Was She. New York:
Neale, 1906.

A New Orleans family is besieged by
wartime privations.

235. Crane, Stephen. The Red Badge of Courage.
     New York: Appleton, 1896.

     A young soldier examines his fears just
     before he fights at the Battle of Chancel-
     lorsville. One of the great classics of war
     literature, this study of courage and valor
     could have taken place during any war.

236. Crane, William D. Andrew Johnson. New
     York: Dodd Mead, 1968.

     A rather conventional biographical novel
     of a much misunderstood President.

237. Creel, Catherine. The Yankee and the Belle.
     New York: Belmont Tower, 1979.

     A mediocre, tiresome romance about a
     plantation woman torn between her loyalty to
     the South and her smoldering passion for a
     Union officer.

238. Crim, Matt. Adventures of a Fair Rebel.
     New York: Charles L. Webster, 1891.

     Dislocations of a Southern family.

239. Cross, Jane T.H. Duncan Adair. Macon, GA:
     Burke, Boykin, 1864.

     Morgan's Raiders ride again.

240. Crowell, Joseph E. The Young Volunteer.
     London: F. Tennyson Neely, 1899.

     Adventures of the New Jersey volunteers.

241. Crozier, Robert Haskins. The Confederate
     Spy. Gallatin, TN: R.B. Harmon, 1866.

     A fantastic tale about the exploits of a
     Confederate hero who goes to Cuba after the
     war is lost.

242. ———. Deep Waters. St. Louis: Farris,
     Smith, n.d.

A Mississippi college man fights at
Manassas and is later imprisoned.

243. Cruse, Mrs. Mary Ann. Cameron Hall.
Philadelphia: Lippincott, 1867.

A pro-Southern romance set in Virginia.

244. Cullinan, Thomas. The Beguiled. New York:
Horizon, 1966.

A Union army deserter is cared for and
then imprisoned by some lascivious Southern
women.

245. ————. The Besieged. New York: Horizon,
1970.

A war-weary band of Union cavalry finds
itself encircled by a superior force of
Confederate militia in an isolated part of
South Carolina. A Union major executes the
brother of an iron-willed Southern girl,
which triggers explosive events.

246. Cummings, Betty Sue. Hew Against the Grain.
New York: Atheneum, 1977.

A Virginia family has members on both
sides. Most have decided that slavery is
evil and support the Union, while others
remain loyal to their native soil. A
sensitive novel about the losses that war
brings in its midst.

247. Cummings, Edward. Marmaduke of Tennessee.
Chicago: McClurg, 1914.

A Tennessee gentleman fights for the Lost
Cause and for the love of a fair maiden.

248. Curtis, George Ticknor. John Charaxes.
Philadelphia: Lippincott, 1889.

A rambling tale of a New England family
caught up in romance, politics and war.

249. Dabney, Virginius. The Story of Don Miff.
Philadelphia: Lippincott, 1886.

Life in antebellum and wartime Virginia.

250. Dahlinger, Charles W. Where the Red Volleys
Poured. New York: Dillingham, 1907.

A German-born Union soldier fights at
Fredericksburg and Gettysburg.

251. Daly, Robert W. Guns of Roman Nose. New
York: Dodd, Mead, 1957.

The role of the Cheyenne Indians in the
war.

252. Danford, H.E. The Trail of the Gray
Dragoon. New York: Harold Vinal, 1928.

A saga of Union soldiers in Virginia who
occupy an inn on Gauley Mountain and tangle
with a spirited Southern girl who hates
Yankees.

253. Darby, Ada Claire. Columbine Susan. New
York: Stokes, 1941.

The wartime adventures of a Colorado
governor's daughter.

254. ————. Look Away, Dixieland. New York:
Stokes, 1941.

A young woman in Lexington, Missouri
volunteers as a nurse in a Union hospital
while most of her friends support the
South.

255. Daringer, Helen F. Mary Montgomery, Rebel.
New York: Harcourt, 1948.

A fourteen-year-old Georgia girl comes to
womanhood during the war and Reconstruction.
She finds love and becomes a writer in a
book called "beautifully and sensitively
written" by the Christian Science Monitor.

256. Davis, Burke. To Appomattox. New York:
Rinehart, 1959.

The war's last nine days.

257. Davis, Caroline E. <u>Andy Hall, the Mission</u>
<u>Scholar in the Army</u>. Boston: Henry Hoyt,
1863.

A pious, religious novel whose hero spends
most of his time trying to convert fellow
soldiers.

258. Davis, Garrett Morrow. <u>Hugh Darnaby, a</u>
<u>Story of Kentucky</u>. Washington, D.C.:
Gibson, 1900.

A young, gentleman-farmer from the
Bluegrass Region of Kentucky joins the
Confederate Army, though his brothers fight
for the Union.

259. Davis, Hazel H. <u>General Jim</u>. Minneapolis:
Bethany, 1950.

Future President James Garfield's exploits
as a Union officer.

260. Davis, John E. <u>Belleview</u>. New York: John
B. Alden, 1889.

A Georgia family saga.

261. Davis, Julia. <u>Bridle the Wind</u>. New York:
Rinehart, 1953.

A wife helps a fugitive slave and flees to
New York to live with her sister, but her
Virginia-born husband comes to fetch her. A
warm-hearted, sentimental love story.

262. Davis, M.E.M. <u>In War Times At La Rose</u>
<u>Blanche</u>. Boston: Lothrop, 1888.

A great old New Orleans house and its
occupants adjust to war.

263. ———. <u>The Price of Silence</u>. Boston:
Houghton Mifflin, 1907.

A love story in Confederate New Orleans
before the Union occupation.

264. Davis, Maggie. *The Far Side of Home*. New
      York: Macmillan, 1963.

      A Confederate soldier marries in haste
      while home on leave. This novel explores
      the commitment of small-town Georgians who
      did not own slaves but who fought willingly
      for the cause.

265. Davis, Norah. *The Northerners*. New York:
      Century, 1905.

      A love story of divided Holmes County,
      Tennessee.

266. Davis, Paxton. *The Seasons of Heroes*. New
      York: Morrow, 1967.

      In 1864, Confederate cavalry engage in
      raids in Pennsylvania.

267. Davis, Samuel Hoffman. *Separated by
      Mountains*. Philadelphia: Dorrance,
      1933.

      A romance between a Virginia Military
      Institute student who serves under Jackson
      and a West Virginia girl who sympathizes
      with the Union and becomes a nurse.

268. DeForest, John William. *Miss Ravenel's
      Conversion from Secession to Loyaty*. New
      York: Harper, 1867.

      A New Orleans belle falls for a Union
      soldier and gradually comes to see the
      errors of the South's ways.

269. Deland, Margaret Wade. *The Kays*. New York:
      Harper, 1926.

      A fanatically pacifist family finds their
      views unpopular in war time. Set in Mrs.
      Deland's "Old Chester."

270. DeLeon, Thomas Cooper. *Craig Nest*. Mobile:
      Gossip Printing Company, 1897.

      Sheridan's Campaign.

271.   ———. John Holden, Unionist. St. Paul:
       Price-McGill, 1893.

       The career of an Alabama mountaineer and
       Unionist scalawag.

272.   Delmar, Vina. Beloved. New York:
       Harcourt, 1956.

       A highly romanticized but vastly
       entertaining portrait of Judah P. Benjamin,
       "the brains of the Confederacy."

273.   Demarest, Phyllis Gordon. The Wilderness
       Brigade. New York: Doubleday, 1956.

       A Union soldier who escapes from a prison
       camp is rescued by a North Carolina family.
       He gets caught up in their tangled lives and
       marries the lady of the manor.

274.   Devon, Louis. Aide To Glory. New York:
       Crowell, 1952.

       An interesting character study of John
       Rawlins, General Grant's aide-de-camp and
       later Secretary of War.

275.   Dial, Joan. Susanna. Greenwich, CT:
       Fawcett, Gold Medal, 1978.

       A sixteen-year-old girl who lives in a
       bordello is forced by a Confederate
       lieutenant to spy for the South in England.
       She is also in love with a strange sailor
       from the C.S.S. Shenandoah.

276.   Dick, Trella Damson. The Island on the
       Border. New York: Abelard-Schuman,
       1963.

       A pro-Union family living in southern
       Missouri takes refuge from Rebel raiders on
       an island in the Missouri River. They help
       escaping slaves and Northern spies.

277.   Dickinson, Anna E. What Answer? Boston:
       Ticknor & Fields, 1868.

Romances and battles from New York to North Carolina.

278. Dickson, Capers. John Ashton. Atlanta: Foote & Davies, 1896.

Dedicated "to the heroes who wore the grey and bravely bore the starry cross," this is a pro-Southern view of the war.

279. Dickson, Harris. The Ravanels. Philadelphia: Lippincott, 1905.

A Natchez family renders distinguished service to the Confederacy.

280. Dillon, Mary. In Old Bellaire. New York: Century, 1906.

A prim, puritanical girl in a quaint Pennsylvania town will not let herself love a daring, handsome Southerner.

281. Divine, Arthur Durham. Thunder On the Chesapeake. New York: Macmillan, 1961.

A romance with the background of the crucial battle between the Monitor and the Merrimac.

Divine, David. see Divine, Arthur

282. [Dixon, Samuel Houston] Robert Warren, the Texan Refugee. Chicago: W.H. Harrison, Jr., 1879.

283. Dixon, Thomas, Jr. The Clansman. New York: Doubleday, 1905.

Dixon was a bizarre figure, a bitter racist and one-time Baptist preacher whose books found a willing audience even among people of the calibre of Woodrow Wilson. The Clansman, like The Leopard's Spots below, was written to glamorize the Ku Klux Klan. All of Dixon's heroes are Southern whites while blacks are portrayed as sub-human. The Klan is depicted as a necessary organization to drive out the carpetbaggers.

Though a leading literary review called it "a very poor and ridiculous novel," the book was popular and became the basis for D.W. Griffith's film Birth of a Nation. Dixon also wrote The Black Hood (Appleton, 1924) and The Sins of the Fathers (Appleton, 1912), set during Reconstruction.

284. ———. The Leopard's Spots. New York: Doubleday, 1902.

A Southern view of life in Reconstruction South Carolina.

285. ———. The Man in Gray. New York: Appleton, 1921.

A romanticized portrait of Lee which held some interest because of the author's storytelling ability.

286. ———. The Southerner. New York: Appleton, 1914.

An absurd attempt to prove that Abraham Lincoln was really a Southern white racist at heart.

287. ———. The Traitor. New York: Doubleday, 1907.

The third and final of the author's Reconstruction trilogy. Set in the foot-hills of North Carolina in the early 1870s.

288. ———. The Victim. New York: Appleton, 1914.

A hagiographic view of Jefferson Davis.

289. Doneghy, Dagmar. The Border. New York: Morrow, 1931.

The adventures of a young mother and her six small sons on the Kansas-Missouri border, showing the bitterness of the war in a frontier region. One reviewer called it "a laudible enterprise that has fallen far short of the mark."

290. Dorsey, Sarah A. Panola, a Tale of
     Louisiana. Philadelphia: T.B. Peterson,
     1877.

     A romantic story of southwestern
     Louisiana, including a portrait of the
     Cherokee Indians who join the Confederate
     Army under General Albert Pike.

291. Douglas, Amanda Minnie. Kathie's Soldiers.
     Boston: Lee & Shepard, 1877.

     Yankees flock to the Grand Army of the
     Republic.

292. Dowdey, Clifford. Bugles Blow No More.
     Boston: Little, Brown, 1937.

     Largely a social history of Richmond
     during the war, this convenional historical
     romance shows the gradual disintegration of
     a great city. Allen Tate thought it was
     "largely a series of minor crises that
     failed to develop."

293. ———. Last Night, the Nightingale. New
     York: Doubleday, 1962.

     A look at Reconstruction Virginia.

294. ———. The Proud Retreat. New York:
     Doubleday, 1953.

     A soldier escorts the Confederate treasury
     to safety after the government flees
     Richmond.

295. ———. Tidewater. Boston: Little, Brown,
     1983.

     Life in Richmond during the war.

296. ———. Where My Love Sleeps. Boston:
     Little, Brown, 1945.

     A young Confederate captain meets and
     romances a mysterious girl on a plantation
     near battle-torn Petersburg in the last year
     of the war.

297. Drago, Harry Sinclair. Stagecoach Kingdom.
      New York: Doubleday, 1943.

      What the West was like during the war.

298. Driver, John Merritte. Americans All.
      Chicago: Forbes, 1911.

      Crowded with characters and historical
      detail, this is a novelistic retelling of
      the war. The author was a friend of
      Jefferson Davis.

299. Dunbar, Paul Laurence. The Fanatics. New
      York: Dodd, Mead, 1901.

      Romance triumphs over politics in a
      divided Ohio town.

300. Dunn, Byron Archibald. Battling For
      Atlanta. Chicago: McClurg, 1900.

      All of Dunn's novels reflect the Union
      position and were written for younger
      readers. Basically they are a retelling of
      major battles with young soldiers from
      Kentucky and Missouri as heroes.

301. ———. The Boy Scouts of the Shenandoah.
      Chicago: McClurg, 1916.

      A Virginia aristocrat and a young mountain
      boy join the Union forces as independent
      scouts.

302. ———. The Courier of the Ozarks.
      Chicago: McClurg, 1912.

303. ———. From Atlanta to the Sea. Chicago:
      McClurg, 1901.

304. ———. General Nelson's Scout. Chicago:
      McClurg, 1898.

305. ———. The Last Raid. Chicago: McClurg,
      1914.

306. ———. On General Thomas's Staff.
      Chicago: McClurg, 1899.

307. ———. Raiding with Morgan. Chicago: McClurg, 1903.

308. ———. The Scout of Pea Ridge. Chicago: McClurg, 1911.

309. ———. Scouting for Sheridan. Chicago: McClurg, 1918.

310. ———. Storming Vicksburg. Chicago: McClurg, 1913.

311. ———. With the Army of the Potomac. Chicago: McClurg, 1917.

312. ———. With Lyon in Missouri. Chicago: McClurg, 1910.

A Northern abolitionist on his way to Kansas is killed by a Missouri mob. His son finds refuge with a wealthy Southern relative in St. Louis, and joins the Union cause when war breaks out.

313. Dwight, Allan. Linn Dickson, Confederate. New York: Macmillan, 1934.

A young soldier recounts his adventures with Lee, Jackson and Stuart.

314. Dykeman, Wilma. The Tall Woman. New York: Holt, 1962.

A strong woman in the North Carolina mountains fights with stubborn courage for a better life after the war ends. Her husband had fought for the Union but her family had remained loyal to the South. This novel has authentic tone and solid regional background but is not great fiction.

315. Earle, Mary Tracy. The Flag on the Hill Top. New York: Houghton Mifflin, 1902.

Set in Illinois this is a novel about Confederate sympathizers, spies and army deserters trying to get home.

316.   Eaton, Jeannette. Lee, the Gallant
        General. New York: Morrow, 1953.

        A biographical novel.

317.   Eberhart, Mignon G. The Bayou Road. New
        York: Random House, 1979.

        A Southern woman and her black friend try
        to keep their elegant home running
        efficiently in New Orleans though her
        brother is dead and father in exile. A
        Yankee major, a former lover, comes to stay.
        Her Southern fiance suggests that she entice
        secrets from the Yankee, who is a liaison
        officer for Grant.

318.   ————. The Cup, the Blade or the Gun. New
        York: Random House, 1961.

        A Connecticut girl marries a Confederate
        officer. While he is away on a confidential
        mission, her life is threatened.

319.   Edgerton, Lucile Selk. Pillars of Gold.
        New York: Knopf, 1941.

        A melodramatic account of the gold rush in
        Arizona during the war.

320.   Edmonds, Walter D. The Big Barn. Boston:
        Little, Brown, 1930.

        A domestic novel of New York village life
        during the war.

321.   ————. Cadmus Henry. New York: Dodd,
        Mead, 1949.

        A seventeen-year-old boy who wants to be a
        soldier ends up as a baloonist for the
        Confederate Army in an amusing tale set in
        the Peninsular Campaign.

322.   Edwards, Amelia. Debenham's Vow. New York:
        Hurst & Blackett, 1870.

        A vivid account of blockade-running in
        Charleston.

323. Edwards, Warren. The War Reporter. New
York: Street & Smith, 1896.

A New York reporter, serving as a Union
spy in his native Kentucky, outsmarts
General Morgan. He also bests a Confederate
rival for the love of a beautiful woman.

324. Eggert, Robert. The Log House Club.
Philadelphia: Winston, 1911.

All about the Home Guards in the Union
Army.

325. Eggleston, George Cary. The Bale Marked
Circle X. Boston: Lothrop, 1902.

Three young Confederate blockade runners
are sent in a sloop on a secret voyage from
Charleston to the Bahamas, conveying
important documents in a bale of cotton.

326. ————. A Captain in the Ranks. New York:
A.S. Barnes, 1904.

Young Virginians try to rebuild their
lives and fortunes in the West after
Appomattox.

327. ————. A Daughter of the South. Boston:
Lothrop, 1905.

A crude romance about a commodore of a
cotton fleet who rescues a woman fleeing
north.

328. ————. Dorothy South. Boston: Lothrop,
1902.

Love, romance and culture in antebellum
Virginia.

329. ————. Evelyn Byrd. Boston: Lothrop,
1904.

Virginians sense defeat as war turns
against them.

330. ———. The Master of Warlock. Boston: Lothrop, 1903.

A romance set in Virginia during the early days of the war.

331. ———. The Warrens of Virginia. New York: Dillingham, 1908.

Northern and Southern families both suffer the effects of the war.

332. Eggleston, Joseph William. Tuckahoe. New York: Neale, 1903.

A portrait of aristocratic Virginians east of the Blue Ridge.

333. Ehle, John. The Time of Drums. New York: Harper, 1970.

Two brothers fight for the South at Chancellorsville and Gettysburg.

334. Eifert, Virginia. New Birth of Freedom. New York: Dodd Mead, 1959.

All about Lincoln's White House years.

335. Eliot, George Fielding. Caleb Pettengill, U.S.N. New York: Messner, 1956.

A Union gunboat commander blockades Southern ports.

336. Epstein, Samuel and Beryl. The Andrews Raid or The Great Locomotive Chase. New York: Coward, McCann, 1956.

Andrews' Raiders fail in their daring exploit.

337. Erdman, Loula Grace. And Many a Voyage. New York: Dodd, Mead, 1960.

The wife of a crusading reporter and later senator from Kansas views a changing nation. The main character is Senator Edmund Ross.

338.   ————. Another Spring. New York: Dodd,
       Mead, 1966.

       Raiders make life miserable for
       Missourians in the cold winter of 1863.

339.   Ernenwein, Leslie. Rebel Yell. New York:
       Dutton, 1948.

       Several bitter Texans carry their rebel
       sentiments to Arizona territory at war's
       end.

340.   Erskine, John. The Start of the Road.   New
       York: Stokes, 1938.

       This is a novel based on Walt Whitman's
       life from 1848 to 1865.   According to this
       fictitious version, Whitman fathered a child
       by an octoroon in New Orleans.   During the
       war years as a nurse in a Washington
       hospital, he searched unsuccessfully for his
       son.   Time called it "inconsequential and
       not very convincing."

341.   Evans, Edna Hoffman. Sunstar and Pepper.
       Chapel Hill: University of North Carolina
       Press, 1947.

       Pepper is a sixteen-year-old Virginia boy
       who left his home to join Jeb Stuart.   With
       his faithful horse, Sunstar, Pepper and
       another boy become personal couriers to the
       general.   The New York Times called this
       young adult novel "a rousing good story."

342.   Everett, Lloyd I. For Maryland's Honor.
       Boston: Christopher, 1922.

       A propaganda novel about Maryland's
       Confederate soldiers, dedicated "to Dixie's
       defenders everywhere."   Author was a racist
       who wrote Our Racial Heritage.

343.   Fairbank, Janet A. The Bright Land.
       Boston: Houghton Mifflin, 1932.

       More of a feminist novel than a Civil War
       one, this is about a New Hampshire-born

woman who plays an important role in wartime Illinois.

344. ———. The Courtlandts of Washington Square. Indianapolis: Bobbs-Merrill, 1922.

Ann Byrne wants to become a nurse and her upperclass family refuses. But she does as she pleases in this vivid and realistic look at domestic life during the war.

345. Fairman, Paula. Southern Rose. Los Angeles: Pinnacle, 1980.

A Southern actress on tour is loved by two soldiers, one Rebel and one Yank.

346. Falconer, William. Bloom and Brier. Montgomery: Joel White, 1870.

A light romance about "the quiet and conscious grandeur of the South."

347. Farrell, Cliff. Trail of the Tattered Star. New York: Doubleday, 1961.

Confederate sympathizers in San Francisco try to induce California to join the Rebel cause.

348. Fast, Howard. Freedom Road. New York: Duell, 1944.

A partisan, passionate and bitter attack on Southern whites during the Reconstruction period. The hero is an illiterate black man who becomes a member of Congress and tries to help his people. After Northern troops are withdrawn, disaster befalls the black community. Liberal critic Diana Trilling called the novel unrealistic because all blacks were depicted as noble and virtuous.

349. Faulkner, William. The Unvanquished. New York: Random House, 1938.

An unbending Mississippi plantation family continues to harass their Union enemies by

52

engaging in guerilla warfare. Seen through
the eyes of a twelve-year-old boy, this is
"a great and convincing picture of the
aftermath of the great conflict."

350. Ferrell, Elizabeth and Margaret. Full of
      Thy Riches. New York: Mill, 1944.

      A romance of a Quaker woman in West
      Virginia, including Copperhead activties and
      a rebel raid on oil wells. Saturday Review
      called this "a harmless package of cliches
      designed expressly for the gift-shop lending
      libraries."

351. Feuille, Frank. The Cotton Road. New York:
      Morrow, 1954.

      A crippled Southern boy joins forces with
      a young Englishman to get cotton through the
      Union blockade of Texas. The New York Times
      said it "combines the flavor of pure
      history, the excitement of high romance and
      international intrigue."

352. Fisher, Clay. The Crossing. Boston:
      Houghton, Mifflin, 1958.

      Northern and Southern cavalry clash in the
      Southwest.

353. Fleming, A.M. A Soldier of the Confederacy.
      Boston: Meador, 1934.

      Dedicated "to those invincible heroes of
      the Confederacy," this is about an east
      Tennessee mountaineer who wore the grey.

354. Fleming, Berry. The Affair at Honey Hill.
      Augusta, GA: Cotton Lane Press, 1981.

355. Floyd, N.J. The Last of the Cavaliers.
      New York: Broadway, 1904.

      A pro-Southern romance about a Virginia
      family on an Alabama plantation.

356. ————. Thorns in the Flesh. New York:
      Hubbard, 1884.

A strident defense of the Southern way of life, it was written specifically to counter Albion Tourgee.

357. Fluker, Anne and Winifred. Confedric Gol. Macon: J.W. Burke, 1926.

358. Fontaine, Francis. Etowah. Atlanta: Privately printed, 1887.

A long, pro-Southern romance almost mythical in texture.

359. Foote, Shelby. Shiloh. New York: Dial, 1952.

The famous battle seen through the eyes of six soldiers. The characters are subordinate to the battle scenes.

360. Ford, Jesse Hill. The Raider. Boston: Little, Brown, 1977.

An epic novel about plantation life in Tennessee.

361. Ford, Sally Rochester. Raids and Romance of Morgan and His Men. New York: Charles B. Richardson, 1864.

A nineteen-year-old Louisville lad rides with Morgan. Richard Harwell calls this "a capstone of Confederate literature."

362. Fordyce, W.C., Jr. Civil War Dragoon. Hicksville, NY: Exposition Press, 1965.

Adventures of a Union cavalry soldier.

363. Forrest, J.R. The Student Cavaliers. New York: R.F. Fenno, 1908.

In a Pennsylvania college the class of 1861 has students who fight for both sides.

Fortis et Fidelis. See May, Thomas P.

364. Fosdick, Charles. Frank Before Vicksburg. Cincinnati: R.W. Carroll, 1866.

365. ————. Frank On a Gunboat. Cincinnati:
      R.W. Carroll, 1864.

366. ————. Frank On the Lower Mississippi.
      Cincinnati: R.W. Carroll, 1867.

367. ————. Marcy the Blockade Runner.
      Philadelphia: Porter & Coates, 1891.

      A Tennessee family living in North
      Carolina really support the Union but must
      present a front to their neighbors. One son
      becomes a lukewarm blockade runner but his
      brother joins the Union fleet.

368. ————. Marcy the Refugee. Philadelphia:
      Porter & Coates, 1892.

      In this sequel Marcy changes sides and
      leads the Union fleet to capture Roanoke
      Island. All of the Fosdick series were
      pro-Union adventure novels for young adult
      readers.

369. ————. Rodney the Overseer. Philadelphia:
      Porter & Coates, 1892.

370. ————. Rodney the Partisan. Philadelphia:
      Porter & Coates, 1890.

371. ————. Sailor Jack the Trader.
      Philadelphia: Porter & Coates, 1893.

372. ————. True To His Colors. Philadelphia:
      Porter & Coates, 1889.

373. Fowler, Robert H. Jim Mundy. New York:
      Harper, 1977.

      Fowler has made the Confederate soldier
      come alive in this reminiscence of an
      elderly veteran.

374. Fox, John, Jr. The Little Shepherd of
      Kingdom Come. New York: Scribner, 1903.

      Love overcomes political and class
      differences when an aristocratic pro-
      Confederate girl from Lexington, Kentucky

marries a homeless mountain boy who supports
the Union.

375. Fraser, George M. <u>Flash for Freedom</u>. New
      York: Knopf, 1972.

      A dashing Englishman gets involved in the
      slave trade and the Civil War.

376. Frederic, Harold. <u>The Copperhead</u>. New
      York: Scribner, 1893.

      A realistic description of how a small
      farming community in upstate New York
      despised, ostracized, and eventually burned
      out the lone dissenter, a man who had once
      been the leading citizen. He opposed the
      Republican-Union cause and paid a price in a
      closed society.

377. ————. <u>The Return of the O'Mahoney</u>. New
      York: Scribner, 1892.

378. Fremont, Jesse Benton. <u>The Story of the</u>
      <u>Guard</u>. Boston: Ticknor and Fields,
      1863.

      Exploits of Zagonyi's Guard in Missouri.

379. French, Alice. <u>Expiation</u>. New York:
      Scribner, 1890.

380. Frothingham, Jessie P. <u>Running the</u>
      <u>Gauntlet</u>. New York: Appleton, 1906.

      A Yankee naval hero destroys a Southern
      ship.

381. Fuller, Edwin Wiley. <u>Sea-Gift</u>. New York:
      E.J. Hale, 1873.

      A sentimental novel of antebellum and
      Civil War North Carolina.

382. Gaither, Frances. <u>Follow the Drinking</u>
      <u>Gourd</u>. New York: Macmillan, 1940.

      An Alabama plantation falls into ruin
      shortly before the war. <u>The New York Times</u>

said it was "compassionate, moving and
written with beautiful simplicity and
economy."

383. Gardener, Helen H. An Unofficial Patriot.
      Boston: Arena Publishing Company, 1894.

      The melodramatic tale of a Southern
      Methodist minister and slave owner.

384. Gardiner, Dorothy. The Great Betrayal. New
      York: Doubleday, 1949.

      The Battle of Sand Creek, Colorado.

385. Garland, Hamlin. Trail-Makers of the
      Middle Border. New York: Macmillan,
      1926.

      A masterly saga of a Maine farmer who
      moved to Wisconsin and fought in the war.

386. Garth, David. Gray Canaan. New York:
      Putnam, 1947.

      A richly detailed description of life in
      Richmond and Washington in the summer of
      1862. Chief characters are a Confederate
      captain and his girl.

387. Gedney, Frederick. Shenandoah. New York:
      T.S. Ogilvie, 1890.

      The last days in Virginia.

388. Gentry, Claude. Crossroads. Baldwyn, MS:
      Magnolia, 1954.

      A Philadelphia man comes to Mississippi
      and falls in love with a beautiful belle.
      But he joins the Union army and his fiance's
      father threatens vengeance. The Yankee is
      seriously wounded and is nursed by his
      beloved. He realizes he had made a mistake
      and joins the Confederate Army, finding that
      his true homeland is Dixie. He returns home
      and sees his newborn son.

389. George, Rebecca. <u>Tender Longing</u>. New York:
     Pocket Books, 1986.

     A romantic mystery about a young woman
     whose Georgia plantation is sacked. She
     falls in love with a Union officer who is
     later charged wrongly with murder. He must
     find the real murderer before she becomes
     the next victim.

     Gildersleeve, Mrs. C.H. See Longstreet,
       Rachel Abigail

390. Giles, Janis Holt. <u>Run Me a River</u>. Boston
     Houghton Mifflin, 1964.

     Riverboat passengers and crew try to
     maintain business as usual despite gunboats
     and naval battles.

391. Gilliam, David Tod. <u>Dick Devereux</u>.
     Cincinnati: Stewart and Kidd, 1915.

     A romance set in central Ohio and the
     Virignia mountains.

392. Gilmore, James Roberts. <u>Among the
       Guerillas</u>. New York: Carleton, 1866.

     More pictures of Southern life in story
     form.

393. ———. <u>Among the Pines</u>. New York:
     Charles T. Evans, 1862.

     Hardly a novel at all, but more of a
     travelogue to the evils of Dixie. It was
     apparently published during the war to stir
     up hatred of the South.

394. ———. <u>A Mountain-White Heroine</u>. New
     York: Belford Clark, 1889.

     A romance of the poor whites, many of whom
     supported the Union, in what the author
     calls the Southern Alleghenies.

395. ———. <u>On the Border</u>. Boston: Lee &
     Shepard, 1867.

James Garfield (later President) and a spy
team up to save Kentucky for the Union.

396. Glasgow, Alice. _Twisted Tendril_. New York:
     Stokes, 1928.

     A sketch of John Wilkes Booth, showing
     that mistaken zeal was his Achilles heel.
     Saturday Review called it "historical
     entertainment of an unusually good kind,"
     while the _New York Herald Tribune_ said the
     author "makes Booth live in her pages."

397. Glasgow, Ellen. _The Battle-Ground_. New
     York: Doubleday, 1902.

     A major novel concentrating on the
     military exploits and strategy.

398. ————. _The Deliverance_. New York:
     Doubleday, 1904.

     Virginia planters struggle to survive
     during the Reconstruction.

399. Glenwood, Ida. _Lilly Pearl and the Mistress
     of Rosedale_. Chicago: Dibble Publishing
     Company, 1892.

     A melodramatic romance of the South.

400. Goede, William. _Quantrill_. Dunvegan,
     Ontario: Quadrant, 1982.

     A biographical novel of the enigmatic
     drifter turned soldier who wreaked terror on
     Unionists and abolitionists.

401. Goff, Mrs. Harriet Newell. _Other Fools and
     Their Doings, or Life Among the Freedmen_.
     New York: Ogilvie, 1880.

     A Southern white view of the horrors of
     black rule and Reconstruction in South
     Carolina.

402. Goodrich, Arthur. _The Sign of Freedom_. New
     York: Appleton, 1916.

Though a farm boy had a cruel life, he becomes a patriot during the war.

403. Gordon, Armistead. <u>Ommirandy</u>. New York: Scribner, 1917.

An ex-slave stays with the family.

404. Gordon, Caroline. <u>None Shall Look Back</u>. New York: Scribner, 1937.

Southern feudal society crumbles under the impact of the war. <u>The New York Times</u> said it "has both distinction and dignity."

405. Gorrell, Joseph R. <u>Sins Absolved</u>. Des Moines: Kenyon Printing Company, 1895.

Experiences of Midwestern soldiers, heavy on war, religion and love.

406. Goss, Warren Lee. <u>In the Navy</u>. New York: Crowell, 1898.

An account of naval battles on the inland waters of Virginia and North Carolina narrated by a North Carolinian Union sailor whose father was a Confederate.

407. ———. <u>Jack Alden</u>. New York: Crowell, 1895.

The Virginia military campaigns.

408. ———. <u>Jed</u>. New York: Crowell, 1889.

Two young men escape from Andersonville down the Flint and Appalachicola Rivers to the Gulf of Mexico.

409. ———. <u>Tom Clifton</u>. New York: Crowell, 1892.

Adventures with Grant and Sherman.

410. Graydon, Nell S. <u>Another Jezebel</u>. Columbia, S.C.: R.L. Bryan, 1958.

Based on a true incident, this is a story
of a beautiful South Carolina woman who was
a Union spy and her extraordinarily lovely
daughter who became a countess after the
war.

411. Greene, Aella. John Peters. Springfield,
MA: Clark W. Bryan, 1891.

Two volume novel about a New England farm
family, some of whose members fought at
Gettysburg.

412. Greene, Homer. A Lincoln Conscript.
Boston: Houghton Mifflin, 1909.

A Copperhead refuses conscription, but he
meets Lincoln and becomes convinced of the
justice of the Union cause.

413. Griswold, Francis. A Sea Island Lady. New
York: Morrow, 1939.

A 964-page chronicle of a Beaufort, South
Carolina family. The heroine is a Northern
girl who marries a local aristocrat and
helps to rebuild his plantation. Catholic
World said, "It is a gargantuan novel but
its size has not made it great."

414. Grubb, Davis. A Dream of Kings. New York:
Scribner, 1955.

An orphan raised by an aunt in West
Virginia joins Stonewall's army and idolizes
him. After the General's death, the young
man deserts, returns home and marries a girl
who shares his dreams.

415. Gruber, Frank. Buffalo Grass. New York:
Rinehart, 1956.

A well-written, fast-moving tale of the
war's closing days in Kansas.

416. ———. The Bushwackers. New York:
Rinehart, 1959.

Quantrill's Raiders massacre Union
supporters in Lawrence, Kansas in 1863.

417. ———. Outlaw. New York: Bantam, 1963.

An embittered Southerner declares a
personal vendetta on Union troops after his
best friend is killed.

418. Guluk, Grover C. A Drum Calls West.
Boston: Houghton Mifflin, 1952.

A Union veteran loves a girl whose father
was a Rebel. Takes place in rough and
tumble Idaho during the war years and
after.

419. Gunter, Archibald C. Billy Hamilton. New
York: Home Publishing Company, 1898.

A Marylander serves the Confederate Army
with honor.

420. Haas, Ben. The Foragers. New York: Simon
& Schuster, 1962.

Taking place in one day, this is a
convincing story of the struggle for
survival as the war nears its close. Class
conflicts are important.

421. Hagan, Patricia. Love and War. New York:
Avon, 1978.

A sultry romance of a Southern woman torn
between Yankee and Rebel lovers.

422. Hall, Anna Gertrude. Cyrus Holt and the
Civil War. New York: Viking, 1964.

A boy in a village in Upstate New York
carefully observes the wartime preparations,
enlistment activities, marching of gaily
dressed Zouaves and tragic news of battlefield deaths. A good homefront novel for
younger readers.

423. Hall, Marjory. Beneath Another Sun.
Philadelphia: Westminster, 1970.

A Southern sympathizer leaves Connecticut
to join the Confederate Army and leaves his
wife and daughters in Richmond. They are
treated cooly, and one of the daughters
cannot understand what she is doing in the
Confederate capital.

424.   ————. The Carved Wooden Ring. Philadel-
         phia: Westminster, 1972.

A frivolous Baltimore woman has lovers on
both sides but she becomes more sympathetic
to the Southern cause as the war progresses.
She becomes a nurse and then a spy and is
banished to Richmond.

425.   Hamilton, E.J. Uncle John and the Army and
        Among Freed Men. New York: American
        Tract Society, 1867.

Religious propaganda disguised as fiction.

426.   Hamilton, Mrs. Sylla Withers. Forsaking All
        Others; a Story of Sherman's March Through
        Georgia. New York: Neale, 1905.

427.   Hanaford, Mrs. P.A. Frank Nelson. Boston:
        William H. Hill, 1866.

A very young New Hampshire boy runs away
to join the Union army.

428.   Hancock, Albert Elmer. Henry Bourland. New
        York: Macmillan, 1901.

The extinction of the Southern aristocracy
and its ideals and traditions.

429.   Hancock, Mary Alice. Menace on the Mountain
        Philadelphia: Macrae Smith, 1968.

Yankee sympathizers populate western North
Carolina. So do bushwackers, who make life
miserable for everyone.

430.   Hancock, Sallie J. The Montanas. New York:
        Carleton, 1866.

Domestic life in rural New Hampshire.

431. Hanford, C.H. General Claxton. New York: Neale, 1917.

A strange mixture of religion, war and romance.

432. Hanna, Elizabeth Heming. High Mountain. New York: Abbey Press, 1902.

An idyll of the Old South.

433. Harben, Will Nathaniel. A Mute Confessor. Boston: Arena, 1892.

How Chattanooga held up during the war.

434. ———. The Triumph. New York: Harper, 1917.

Two Georgia brothers differ in their views of slavery. Andrew, who opposes it, is ostracized by family and community. His brother, Thomas, plantation owner, becomes a Confederate brigadier general. Andrew is forced to flee and barely survives but joins the Union army. When he returns home before the war's end, his unwise behavior makes him more despised than ever. The New York Times said, "It contains many of the elements that make for greatness."

435. Hargis, Thomas F. A Patriot's Strategy. Louisville: Charles T. Dearing, 1895.

A love story of a Confederate soldier and a Northern girl who nurses him in a Louisville hospital.

Harland, Marion. See Terhune, Mary Virginia

436. Harper, Frances Ellen Watkins. Iola Leroy, or Shadows Uplifted. Boston: Earle, 1895.

A wealthy planter married a young slave, but their daughter is sold into slavery when he dies. She is brought to North Carolina but escapes to serve as a Union nurse.

Harrington, George F. See Baker, William
Mumford

437. Harris, Joel Chandler. Gabriel Tolliver.
New York: McClure, Phillips, 1902.

Blacks try to adjust to their new freedom
in postwar years while many whites seek
refuge in the Klan.

438. ———. A Little Union Scout. New York:
McClure Phillips, 1904.

A lovely female disguises herself as a
Union scout.

439. ———. On the Plantation. New York:
Appleton, 1892.

A semi-autobiographical portrait of a
Georgia boy's adventures during the war.

440. ———. The Shadow Between His Shoulder
Blades. Boston: Small, Maynard, 1909.

It's an almost unreadable dialect novel
about a Confederate soldier.

441. Harris, Leon F. and Frank Beals. Look Away,
Dixieland. New York: Speller, 1937.

The sad plight of a returned soldier in
Reconstruction Mississippi who finds his
wife dead and plantation on the brink of
ruin. He is unable to adjust but his
courageous daughter saves the day.

442. Harrison, Constance Cary (Mrs. Burton).
The Carlyles. New York: Appleton, 1905.

A detailed account of the evacuation of
Richmond. A Union officer protects the
Carlyles' home because of his love for a
Southern girl. President Lincoln appears as
a character.

443. ———. Flower de Hundred. New York:
Cassell, 1890.

The story of a Virginia plantation and its denizens.

444. Harrison, Ida Withers. Beyond the Battle's Rim. New York: Neale, 1918.

A Mississippi family is caught up in romance and battles. Even the preacher joins up.

445. Harrison, W.S. Sam Williams. Nashville: Methodist Episcopal Church, 1892.

A sympathetic assessment of life in the Old South.

446. Hart, Scott. Eight April Days. New York: Coward, 1949.

The retreat of the Confederates from Petersburg to Appomattox as experienced by an old woman peddler. On the way she gives courage to a deserter and helps a confused couple. Reviewers found it impressive and unpretentious.

447. Harte, Bret. Clarence. Boston: Houghton Mifflin, 1895.

A California industrialist who becomes a Union general tries to restrain his staunchly Southern wife.

448. Havighurst, Marion Boyd. The Sycamore Tree. New York: World, 1960.

Families and friendships are destroyed by wartime passions. Set in Ohio.

449. Hawkins, Willis B. Andy Barr. Boston: Lothrop, 1903.

A small, Illinois town rallies to the Union.

450. Haycox, Ernest. The Long Storm. Boston: Little, Brown, 1946.

A vivid, tough and realistic portrait of a Copperhead organization operating in

Portland, Oregon. They are thwarted by a
ship captain.

451. Haydn, Ruff. Pine Mountain Americans. New
York: Hobson, 1947.

The trials and hardships of a married
couple and their friends in Faulkner County,
Arkansas.

452. Haynes, Betsy. Cowslip. Nashville:
Nelson, 1973.

A thirteen-year-old black girl named
Cowslip is sold at an auction in Kentucky in
1861. She and her fellow slaves dream of
freedom, and several try to escape during
the war and head for Canada.

453. Haynes, Emory James. A Wedding In War-Time.
Boston: James H. Earle, 1890.

A didactic romance written by the pastor
of Tremont Temple in Boston.

454. Hayward, William Stephens. The Black Angel.
London: Charles H. Clarke, 1868.

It's a long digressive romance.

455. ———. The Star of the South. London:
Charles H. Clarke, n.d.

Sequel to The Black Angel.

Hazel, Harry. See Jones, Justin

456. Heagney, Harold Jerome. Blockade Running.
New York: Longmans, 1939.

The adventures of John Bannister Tabb on a
Confederate blockade runner.

457. Hebson, Ann. The Latimer Legend. New York:
Macmillan, 1961.

The diary of a woman serving with Morgan's
Raiders reveals the war's progress in West
Virginia.

458. Heidish, Marcy. A Woman Named Moses.
     Boston: Houghton, Mifflin, 1976.

     Maryland's Harriet Tubman comes to life as
     she overcomes slavery and oppression.

459. Henderson, LeGrand. Glory Horn. New York:
     McBride, 1941.

     A young Georgian fights to keep his
     plantation going, hunts a stolen fortune in
     cotton, and battles the Union Army in
     Virginia. His family fights Sherman back in
     Georgia.

460. Henkle, Henrietta. Deep River. New York:
     Harcourt, 1944.

     An anti-slavery mountaineer in Georgia
     opposes slavery and supports the Union, even
     though his wife was raised on a plantation.
     The New York Times said it was a novel "in
     which events have moral values."

     Henry, Will. See Allen, Henry

461. Henty, George Alfred. With Lee in Virginia.
     London: Blackie, 1890.

     The early Confederate triumphs seen by a
     young recruit.

462. Hergesheimer, Joseph. The Limestone Tree.
     New York: Knopf, 1931.

     The saga of a Kentucky family from the
     late 18th to the late 19th centuries. Of it
     The New York Times wrote: "Richly and
     powerfully American, a carefully done epic
     drama, skillfully varying its artistry."

463. Heyward, DuBose. Peter Ashley. New York:
     Farrar, 1932.

     A Charleston aristocrat has just returned
     from Oxford as South Carolina secedes. He
     opposes secession but eventually gives in
     and fights for the South. One reviewer
     called it "a costume drama in the most

spectacular and finest sense of the word."
Its descriptions of Charleston life are
considered masterful.

464. Hiatt, James M. The Test of Loyalty.
Indianapolis: Merrill & Smith, 1864.

Designed as Union propaganda and as an
attack on Northern Democrats, this novel
shows the plight of Union supporters in
Tennessee.

465. Hickman, Janet. Zoar Blue. New York:
Macmillan, 1978.

A fascinating, well-told tale of how the
war changed an isolated community of German
Separatists - a pacifist religious group
which settled on farms in remote Zoar, Ohio.
Contrary to their upbringing, several young
men join the Union Army and fight at
Gettysburg. When they return home, their
perceptions of life have changed.

466. Hicks, John. The Long Whip. New York:
McKay, 1969.

Black soldiers serve the Union but find
life little changed in postwar Dixie.

467. Hill, Alonzo F. John Smith's Funny
Adventures on a Crutch. Philadelphia:
John E. Potter, 1869.

The humorous escapades of a one-legged
soldier.

468. Hilles, Lewis Baker. Chickens Come Home to
Roost. New York: Isaac H. Blanchard,
1899.

This story of a noble Virginian from
Culpeper County degenerates into a soap
opera.

469. Hincks, Elizabeth Eaton. Undismayed; The
Story of a Yankee Chaplain's Family in the
Civil War. Otis, MA: Privately Printed,
1952.

A religiously oriented home-front novel.

470. Hinkins, Virginia. Stonewall's Courier.
New York: McGraw-Hill, 1959.

A sixteen-year-old Virginia boy runs away
from home and becomes a courier for
Stonewall during the desperate Shenandoah
campaign. He is ordered back to school by
the general.

471. Hinman, Wilbur F. Corporal Si Klegg and His
Pard. Cleveland: N.G. Hamilton, 1889.

Rambunctious, humorous memoirs of Union
soldiers.

472. Hoehling, Mary D. Girl Soldier and Spy.
New York: Messner, 1959.

A young woman becomes a Union spy in
Virginia.

473. ————. Thaddeus Love, America's One-Man
Air Corps. New York: Messner, 1958.

A biographical novel about a balloonist
who developed aerial reconnaissance for the
Union.

474. Hogan, Ray. The Ghost Rider. New York:
Pyramid, 1960.

Mosby's Rangers capture a Union general.

475. ————. Hell to Hallelujah. New York:
Macfadden, 1962.

A small group of Confederate guerillas
battles Yankee troops and renegades.

476. ————. Mosby's Last Ride. New York:
Macfadden, 1966.

The intrepid Confederate's last mission.

477. ————. Night Raider. New York: Avon,
1964.

Mosby and his followers take another important Union figure.

478.   ———. Rebel Ghosts. New York: Macfadden, 1964.

The Yankees finally capture the elusive John Singleton Mosby.

479.   ———. Rebel Raid. New York: Berkeley, 1961.

Southerners embark on a dangerous mission to rescue a young woman spy.

480.   Holmes, Mary Jane. Hugh Worthington. New York: Carleton, 1865.

A Kentucky anti-slavery man serves in the Union Army and moves to Connecticut after the war.

481.   ———. Rose Mather. New York: Carleton, 1868.

A small Northern town feels the effects of war.

482.   Honig, Donald. Walk Like a Man. New York: William Sloane, 1961.

A young Long Island boy comes of age as he searches for a friend accused of being a Rebel spy.

483.   Hooper, Byrd. Beef for Beauregard. New York: Putnam, 1959.

Young Texans search for food supplies for starving Confederate forces.

484.   Hoover, Francis T. Enemies in the Rear. Boston: Arena Publishing, 1895.

The pro-Southern Knights of the Golden Circle operates in southeastern Pennsylvania.

485. Hopkins, Herbert M. The Fighting Bishop. Indianapolis: Bowen-Merrill, 1902.

A Northern Episcopalian bishop's three sons have gone off to war.

486. Horan, James David. Seek Out and Destroy. New York: Crown, 1958.

A Confederate naval vessel goes halfway around the world to destroy Yankee whaling ships.

487. Horsley, Reginald. The Blue Balloon, a Tale of the Shenandoah Valley. New York: Dutton, 1896.

A Staunton, Virginia boy fights for Stonewall.

488. ———. Stonewall's Scout. New York: Harper, 1896.

A Confederate view of the battles of Antietam and Gettysburg.

489. Hosmer, George W. As We Went Marching On. New York: Harper, 1885.

A Union soldier's adventures.

490. Hosmer, James Kendall. The Thinking Bayonet. Boston: Walker, Fuller, 1865.

A University man gets involved in the war in a boring novel that never goes anywhere.

491. Hough, Emerson. The Way of a Man. New York: Orting, 1907.

A wartime romance in the valley of Virginia.

492. Howard, Frances Thomas. In and Out of the Lines. New York; Neale, 1905.

Sherman in Georgia.

493. Howard, John Hamilton. <u>In the Shadow of the</u>
     <u>Pines</u>. New York: Eaton & Mains, 1906.

     An emissary from the French emperor is
     murdered in Virginia's Dismal Swamp.

494. Howard, Oliver Otis. <u>Henry in the War</u>.
     Boston: Lee & Shepard, 1899.

     A boy from Upstate New York becomes a
     model volunteer and sees action in five
     major battles. He survives and marries his
     sweetheart. He is very religious and
     justifies a Christian's fighting and
     killing.

495. Howe, Mary Ann. <u>The Rival Volunteers</u>. New
     York: John Bradburn, 1864.

     A silly, Victorian romance with a little
     war thrown in.

496. Hoy, Mrs. Frank L. <u>Adrienne</u>. New York:
     Neale, 1906.

     A love story with a happy ending set on
     the Gulf Coast.

497. Hubbard, Freeman H. <u>Vinnie Ream and Mr.</u>
     <u>Lincoln</u>. New York: McGraw-Hill, 1949.

     A seventeen-year-old girl models Lincoln
     at the White House. After his death she is
     chosen as sculptress for his marble statue
     in the Capitol Rotunda. Based on fact, an
     exciting tale of Washington during the war.

498. Hughes, Rupert. <u>The Whirlwind</u>. Boston:
     Lothrop, 1902.

     Southern family life is unalterably
     changed.

499. Hunt, Irene. <u>Across Five Aprils</u>. Chicago:
     Follett, 1964.

     A Southern Illinois farm boy grows up
     during the war.

500. Hunt, Mabel Leigh. <u>Lucinda, a Little Girl</u>
     <u>of 1860</u>. Philadelphia: Lippincott,
     1934.

     A gentle, sentimental tale in which a
     little girl awakens to the realities of
     slavery and war.

501. Hutchens, Jane. <u>John Brown's Cousin</u>. New
     York: Doubleday, 1940.

     Henry Brown, son of a Missouri pioneer,
     saw a man killed in a duel and vowed never
     to take a life. During the war he fled to
     Canada and was ostracized upon his return.
     A good portrait of a stubborn non-
     conformist.

502. ————. <u>Timothy Larkin</u>. New York:
     Doubleday, 1942.

     A Missouri family's amazing adventures
     from 1851 to 1861. During the war the
     father saves his son's life.

503. Icenhower, Joseph B. <u>The Scarlet Raider</u>.
     Philadelphia, Chilton, 1961.

     A sixteen-year-old joins Mosby's Rangers.

504. Ingraham, Ellen. <u>Bond and Free</u>.
     Indianapolis: C.B. Ingraham, 1882.

     The injustice of slavery and the plight of
     the Quadroons is the theme of this novel.

505. Jacob, Helen Pierce. <u>The Diary of the</u>
     <u>Strawbridge Place</u>. New York: Atheneum,
     1978.

     A Quaker father, involved in Underground
     Railroad activities, has the loyal support
     of one daughter but the opposition of a twin
     sister.

506. Jacobs, Thornwell. <u>Red Lanterns on St.</u>
     <u>Michaels</u>. New York: Dutton, 1940.

A long, historically accurate portrait of
Charleston during the war, but plot and
characters are weak. Saturday Review said
it "creaks with Victorian melodrama."

507. ————. When for the Truth. Charleston,
S.C.: Walker, Evans and Cogswell, 1950.

New hatreds poison life in Reconstruction
South Carolina.

508. Jakes, John. Love and War. New York:
Harcourt, 1984.

509. ————. North and South. New York:
Harcourt, 1982.

A colorful saga of the long friendships
between a Southern family and a Northern
family which withstood the hatreds of
wartime.

510. ————. The Texans Ride North.
Minneapolis: Winston, 1952.

Texas troops fight at Manassas.

511. ————. The Titans. New York: Pyramid,
1976.

The Kent family, rich and powerful, is
divided as three sons fight for the South
while the father is a journalist for a
Northern paper.

512. James, T.P. Under Fire. New York: Street
and Smith, 1896.

Tale of the Shenandoah Valley.

John, Alix. See Jones, Alice

513. Johnson, C.F. A Hand Raised at Gettysburg.
Milwaukee: Bruce, 1950.

Lee's invasion of the Keystone State
fails.

514. Johnson, Gerald W. _By Reason of Strength_.
     New York: Minton Balch, 1930.

     A generational saga of Scottish immigrants
     in North Carolina. Includes only a little
     Civil War action.

515. Johnson, Quinn. _The Black Magnolia_. New
     York: Exposition Press, 1958.

     An Alabama woman defends her plantation at
     all costs. A proud black man aids her out
     of gratitude to her father who had freed
     him.

516. Johnston, Mary. _Cease Firing_. Boston:
     Houghton Mifflin, 1912.

     A sequel to _The Long Roll_. _Book Review
     Digest_ called it "a panoramic view of the
     movement of armies and an exquisitely
     beautiful story of love that is stronger
     than death."

517. ———. _The Long Roll_. Boston: Houghton
     Mifflin, 1911.

     A Confederate captain's character is
     strengthened in the heat of battle.
     Reviewers loved it and _Book Review Digest_
     said it "has an epic quality that ensures
     permanence."

518. ———. _Michael Forth_. New York: Harper,
     1919.

     The war dominates the lives of Virginia
     plantation dwellers and even the postwar
     years do not bring them peace.

519. ———. _Miss Delicia Allen_. Boston:
     Little, Brown, 1933.

     A vivid and charming portrait of life on a
     Virginia plantation before and during the
     war.

520. Johnston, Norma. _Of Time and Of Seasons_.
     New York: Atheneum, 1975.

A young adult novel about family life during the war.

521. Johnstone, Herrick. Sargeant Slasher; or the Border Feud. Glasgow: Cameron and Ferguson, n.d.

Union men operate in east Tennessee and north Georgia.

522. Jones, Alice. The Night-Hawk. New York: Stokes, 1901.

Blockade running, spies and strong Southern women.

523. Jones, Douglas C. The Barefoot Brigade. New York: Holt, 1982.

The common soldiers from Arkansas perform with valour through many battles.

524. ————. Elkhorn Tavern. New York: Holt, 1980.

Arkansas farmers die in a bloody battle. The New York Times said it "has the beauty of Shane and the elegiac dignity of Red River."

525. Jones, Justin. Virginia Graham. Boston: Loring, 1868.

An Illinois woman is a Union spy in Mississippi.

526. Jordan, Jan. Dim the Flaring Lamps. Englewood Cliffs: Prentice-Hall, 1972.

A biographical novel of John Wilkes Booth based on thorough historical research.

527. Joseph, R.F. Odile. New York: Ballantine, 1977.

The romance of a New Orleans plantation owner and her persistent Yankee lover.

528. Kaler, James O. With Grant at Vicksburg.
     New York: Burt, 1910.

529. ————. With Sherman to the Sea. New York:
     Burt, 1911.

     A young Union soldier sees action in two
     great campaigns.

530. Kane, Harnett. Bride of Fortune. New York:
     Doubleday, 1948.

     A warm, human portrait of Mrs. Jefferson
     Davis which glamorizes the Southern cause.

531. ————. Gallant Mrs. Stonewall. New York:
     Doubleday, 1957.

     A sympathetic sketch of Stonewall
     Jackson's wife that reads more like fact
     than fiction.

532. ————. Lady of Arlington. New York:
     Doubleday, 1953.

     Mary Custis defies her parents and marries
     a poor man who becomes the Confederacy's
     beloved hero. A sense of period and
     background authentically presented.

533. ————. The Smiling Rebel. New York:
     Doubleday, 1955.

     An ably documented action-filled account
     of Confederate spy Belle Boyd.

534. Kane, James J. Ilian. Philadelphia:
     Lippincott, 1888.

     A beautiful Southern spy captivates all
     she meets in this unusual psychological
     tale.

535. Kantor, MacKinlay. Andersonville. New
     York: World Publishing Company, 1955.

     A Pulitzer Prize-winning bestseller about
     the misery and despair in the infamous
     Confederate prison in south Georgia. The

hero is a humane planter on whose property
the prison is built. Bruce Catton and Henry
Steele Commager both thought this was the
greatest Civil War novel of all time.
Saturday Review called it "a kind of
literary Fort Knox."

536.   ————. Arouse and Beware. New York:
        Coward McCann, 1936.

Two Union soldiers escape from Belle
Island Prison in 1864. As they try to reach
Northern lines, they are joined by a woman
fleeing Richmond. A love triangle develops
and the novel becomes somewhat psychological
as well as realistic.

537.   ————. Long Remember. New York: Coward
        McCann, 1934.

In 1863 a young Midwesterner returns to
his former home in Gettysburg, where he has
a love affair with the wife of a friend who
is away at war. Guilt at his non-
involvement consumes him and he enlists.
Vivid, powerful and meritorious, with the
Battle of Gettysburg a major incident.

538.   Kaye-Smith, Sheila. The Challenge to
        Sirius. London: Nixbet, 1917.

A heroic view of the Southern cause,
including scenes at Shiloh, Vicksburg,
Chattanooga, and Missionary Ridge.

539.   Keenan, Henry F. The Iron Game. New York:
        Appleton, 1891.

A college is divided by war. The hero,
who fights for the Union, is accused of a
crime but is acquitted.

540.   Keith, Harold. Rifles for Watie. New York:
        Crowell, 1957.

A Kansas farm boy fighting for the Union
comes up against a Cherokee Indian band
supporting the South.

541. Kelland, Clarence Budington. *Arizona*. New
     York: Harper, 1939.

     A spirited female's adventures in wartime
     Arizona occupy a book the *New Yorker* labeled
     "good old hokum in cowboy dress."

542. Kelley, Evelyn Owens. *Seeded Furrows*.
     Datona Beach, FL: College Publishing,
     1957.

     A tale of Reconstruction Georgia.

543. Kelly, Caroline E. *Andy Hall*. Boston:
     Henry Hoyt, 1863.

544. Kelly, Eleanor Mercein. *Richard Walden's
     Wife*. Indianapolis: Bobbs, Merrill,
     1950.

     Marylanders carry Southern sentiments to
     Wisconsin.

545. Kelso, Isaac. *The Stars and Bars*. Boston:
     Williams, 1863.

     A denunciation of the "reign of terror" of
     Confederate sympathizers in Missouri.

546. Keneally, Thomas. *Confederates*. New York:
     Harper, 1980.

     A wonderful portrait of the poor white
     soldiers who formed the backbone of the
     Confederate army. *Newsweek* said: "It has a
     stunning impact of reality; it's as if the
     veil of history were ripped away and our
     senses drenched by the actions of living
     people at the extremity of human
     experience."

547. Kennedy, Sara Beaumont. *Cicely*. New York:
     Doubleday, 1911.

     A romance set in Georga during the burning
     of Atlanta and Sherman's March.

548. Kennelly, Ardyth. *The Spur*. New York:
     Messner, 1951.

As John Wilkes Booth is dying, he thinks back over his brief twenty-six-year life.

549. Kennerly, S.J. The Story of Sam Tag. New York: Cosmopolitan, 1911.

A ten-year-old boy on a Tennessee planta-tion narrates the progress of the war through his young eyes. His father is the only Union supporter in the district. The real hero is Aunt Betsy, a black mammy who loved the family and chose to stay after the war.

550. Kenyon, Theda. Black Dawn. New York: Messner, 1944.

Yankee schoolteachers tangle with the Klan in Reconstruction Virginia.

551. Key, Alexander. Island Light. Indianapolis: Bobbs-Merrill, 1950.

A Confederate sea-raider escapes from Fort Jefferson in Florida's Dry Tortugas. He reaches his home at Apalachicola and finds that the Reconstruction has changed its way of life.

552. Keyes, Frances Parkinson. The Chess Players. New York: Farrar, 1960.

Paul Morphy, world famous chess player from New Orleans, may also be a Confederate spy in Paris.

553. ————. Madame Castel's Lodger. New York: Farrar, 1962.

General Pierre Beauregard returns to a lonely existence after the war.

554. King, Charles. Between the Lines. New York: Harper, 1888.

A Union soldier carries out his mission with dedication.

555.   ————.   A Broken Sword.   New York: Hobart,
       1905.

       McClellan's Antietam campaign.

556.   ————.   From School to Battlefield.
       Philadelphia, Lippincott, 1899.

       A schoolboy enlists in the Union cause.

557.   ————.   The General's Double.
       Philadelphia: Lippincott, 1897.

       A young man poses as McClellan during the
       advance on Antietam.

558.   ————.   The Iron Brigade.   New York:
       Dillingham, 1902.

       Military exploits of one of Grant's units.

559.   ————.   Kitty's Conquest.   New York:
       Harper, 1884.

       A lawyer falls in love while the Klan
       begins its activities in Reconstruction New
       Orleans.

560.   ————.   A Knight of Columbia.   New York:
       Hobart, 1904.

       The Union cavalry fights in Virginia.

561.   ————.   The Medal of Honor.   New York:
       Hobart, 1905.

       A young Union soldier wins the
       Congressional Medal of Honor for bravery.

562.   ————.   Norman Holt.   New York:
       Dillingham, 1901.

       Exploits of the Army of the Cumberland.

563.   ————.   The Rock of Chickamauga.   New York:
       Dillingham, 1907.

       Heroic portrait of General George Thomas.

564. ———. <u>Trials of a Staff Officer</u>.
Philadelphia: Lippincott, 1896.

A Union Army officer's tribulations.

565. ———. <u>A War-Time Wooing</u>. New York:
Harper, 1888.

A Union officer has a tough time in love
and war.

Kirke, Edmund. See Gilmore, James Roberts

566. Kirkland, Joseph. <u>The Captain of Company
K</u>. Chicago: Dibble, 1891.

A soldier becomes disillusioned by
slackards and war profiteers on the
homefront while soldiers suffer privations.

567. Kjelgaard, James Arthur. <u>The Land Is
Bright</u>. New York: Dodd, Mead, 1958.

A Virginia aristocrat, reluctantly drawn
into the war, falls in love with the wife of
one of his mountaineer troops. <u>Kirkus</u>
called it "a spellbinder and a fine period
piece."

568. Knipe, Emilie Benson and Arthur Alden.
<u>Girls of '64</u>. New York: Neale, 1918.

A Southern colonel's family becomes aware
of "Red Strings," local people in their
Washington, Georgia community who secretly
favor the Union. The traitors communicate
with bits of red colored cloth.

569. Knox, Rose B. <u>Gray Caps</u>. New York:
Doubleday, 1933.

One of the best written and researched
books for younger readers, this recounts the
story of two twin boys from a great South
Carolina plantation who wear the grey.

570. Knox, Thomas W. <u>The Lost Army</u>. New York:
Merriam, 1894.

Two Iowa boys fight for the Union in
Missouri and Arkansas.

571.   Krapp, George Phillip. <u>Sixty Years Ago</u>.
       Chicago: Rand McNally, 1927.

       A Union soldier writes letters to his two
       children from the battlefront.

572.   Krey, Laura L. <u>And Tell of Time</u>. Boston:
       Houghton, Mifflin, 1938.

       A massive novel of Texas during the
       Reconstruction featuring an ex-Confederate
       soldier and his Georgia-born wife. <u>The
       Nation</u> described it as "a conventional if
       ambitious historical romance based on a
       slightly shopworn Southern point of view."

573.   Kroll, Harry Harrison. <u>The Keepers of the
       House</u>. Indianapolis: Bobbs-Merrill,
       1940.

       The illegitimate son of a Mississippi
       plantation owner, rebellious and bitter,
       helps Yankees burn the mansion. Later, he
       gains possession when his paternity is
       acknowledged.

574.   Krout, Caroline Virginia. <u>Knights in
       Fustian</u>. Boston: Houghton Mifflin,
       1900.

575.   Lagard, Garald. <u>Leaps the Live Thunder</u>.
       New York: Morrow, 1955.

       In May 1863 a man and his cat, Colonel
       Turpentine, ride toward Rome, Georgia to
       join General Forrest. The hero joins and
       meets a dancer whom he had spirited from
       Nassau when he was a blockade runner. She
       is part of a traveling tent show owned by a
       lion tamer who loves her. An uproarious
       farce.

576.   ————. <u>Scarlet Cockerel</u>. New York:
       Morrow, 1948.

A Confederate surgeon fighting for Mosby engages in a dangerous romance with the daughter of a Union general.

577. Lancaster, Bruce. **Bride of a Thousand Cedars**. New York: Stokes, 1934.

Blockade-running activities affect life in Bermuda.

578. ———. **Night March**. Boston: Little, Brown, 1958.

The saga of two cavarly captains who tried to free Union prisoners in Richmond, were captured, escaped and fled to Tennessee. The **Chicago Tribune** called it "a pretty good horse opera superimposed on Civil War background."

579. ———. **No Bugles Tonight**. Boston: Little, Brown, 1948.

An absorbing tale of a Northern officer and spy and a Southern woman who aids the Union.

580. ———. **Roll Shenandoah**. Boston: Little, Brown, 1956.

A suspenseful romantic tale of Sheridan's Valley Campaign. The hero, honorably discharged after being wounded, returns to action as a reporter for a New York paper.

581. ———. **The Scarlet Patch**. Boston: Little, Brown, 1947.

Foreign-born volunteers fight for the Union in the war's early days.

582. Lancaster, William Joseph. **Blue and Grey**. New York: Cassell, 1908.

Blockade running and naval battles for younger readers.

583. Landing, W. Frank. **War Cry of the South**. New York: Exposition Press, 1958.

Adventures aboard the <u>Albemarle</u> near Plymouth.

584. Lanier, Sidney. <u>Tiger Lillies</u>. New York: Hurd & Houghton, 1867.

Incisive description of war's horrors with many realistic battle scenes.

585. LaScola, Ray. <u>The Creole</u>. New York: Morrow, 1961.

A sentimental tale about the rich in Reconstruction New Orleans.

586. Lawson, John. <u>The Spring Rider</u>. New York: Crowell, 1968.

A fantasy in which a country boy and his sister, who live near one of the battle-fields, see the ghosts of a Yankee soldier from Maine, a Southern colonel, Stonewall Jackson and Abraham Lincoln.

587. LeCato, N.J.W. <u>Tom Burton</u>. Chicago: Belford Clark & Company, 1888.

Virginians are confident and exuberant in 1861. In this romance nuns make a brief appearance, though they are almost totally absent from Civil War fiction, despite the important role they played in nursing.

588. Leekley, John. <u>The Blue and the Grey</u>. New York: Dell, 1982.

Based on a teleplay this is a story of how two families endured America's darkest war.

589. LeMay, Alan. <u>By Dim and Flaring Lamps</u>. New York: Harper, 1962.

Bands of local guerillas make life precarious for two lovers in Missouri.

590. Lentz, Perry. <u>The Falling Hills</u>. New York: Scribner, 1967.

A Confederate officer from Tennessee and a Boston idealist who commands Negro soldiers at Fort Pillow, Tennessee clash during the Fort Pillow massacre. Best Sellers said it "has marks of incipient greatness."

591.   ————. It Must Be Now the Kingdom Coming. New York: Crown, 1973.

A Union patrol raids a plantation.

592.   Leonard, Mary Hall. The Days of the Swamp Angel. New York: Neale, 1914.

A well written story of social and family life in Charleston.

593.   Levy, Mimi Cooper. Corrie and the Yankee. New York: Viking, 1959.

A little black girl lives on a Southern plantation which is constantly being patrolled after Yankees escape from a local prison.   Her father is a scout for the Union Army.

594.   Lincoln, Jeanie Thomas. Marjorie's Guest. New York: Osgood, 1872.

A brave young girl's adventures, including riding twenty miles through a Southern forest at night to save the life of a Union soldier suspected of being a spy.

595.   Lincoln, Joseph. Storm Signals.   New York: Appleton, 1935.

Blockade runners and sea battles off the Cape Cod coast are the settings for a novel about the relationship between two strongly opinionated sea captains.

596.   Lincoln, Natalie Sumner. The Lost Despatch. New York: Appleton, 1913.

A lovely Southerner who swore allegiance to the Confederacy as her father lay dying is a spy in Washington.   She falls into danger when a dispatch containing vital information for Richmond disappears, and she is arrested for treason and murder.

Lintner, Grace. See Ingraham, Ellen

597. Lloyd, John Uri. Our Willie. Cincinnatti: Kidd, 1934.

A young Kentuckian wins respect after he joins Morgan's Raiders.

598. ————. Stringtown on the Pike. New York: Dodd, Mead, 1900.

A romance set in northern Kentucky.

599. ————. Warwick of the Knobs. New York: Dodd, Mead, 1901.

A stern Baptist minister loses two sons in Morgan's cavalry. His unhappy remaining son also joins, hoping to die.

600. Lockridge, Ross, Jr. Raintree County. Boston: Houghton Mifflin, 1947.

An epic describing the fourth of July in 1892 in the life of an Indiana man. Celebrating with two boyhood friends, he relives his life, including Civil War experiences, in a series of flashbacks. This 1,066-page novel is "an achievement of art and purpose, a cosmically brooding book full of significance and beauty," according to The New York Times.

601. Long, John Luther. War. Indianapolis: Bobbs-Merrill, 1913.

A North-South romance in a divided town. Even the local church was divided, with Southerners on one side, Yankees on the other, and the aisle was called Kentucky.

602. Long, Laura. Without Valor. New York: Longmans, 1940.

An Indiana boy cares for the family mill while his father is away at war.

603. Longstreet, Mrs. Rachel Abigail. Remy St.
     Remy. New York: James O'Kane, 1866.

     A woman disguises herself as a Union
     soldier.

604. Longstreet, Stephen. Gettysburg. New York:
     Farrar, 1961.

     An episodic novel about life on the
     homefront, concentrating on various love
     affairs.

605. ———. Three Days. New York: Messner,
     1947.

     A detailed account of a military strategy
     and carnage at the battle of Gettysburg.

606. Love, Edmund G. An End to Bugling. New
     York: Harper, 1963.

     In this fantasy-satire, General Jeb Stuart
     and his cavalry return to Gettysburg in 1963
     to refight the battle they lost a century
     before.

607. ———. A Shipment of Tarts. New York:
     Doubleday, 1967.

     A delightfully humorous novel about the
     Union Army's evacuation of some prostitutes
     from Memphis.

608. Lowden, Leone. Proving Ground. New York:
     McBride, 1946.

     An Indiana family survives the war and
     fights in many battles.

609. Lytle, Andrew. The Long Night.
     Indianapolis: Bobbs-Merrill, 1936.

     A young man seeks revenge on an under-
     ground terrorist group in Alabama which had
     murdered his father. The Battle of Shiloh
     is a major incident.

610. MacGowan, Alice. The Sword in the
     Mountains. New York: Putnam, 1910.

A look at the suffering and horror of war around Chattanooga and the Cumberland Mountains. The hero is a Confederate officer whose father is pro-Union.

611. Mackie, Pauline Bradford. The Washingtonians. Boston: Page, 1902.

Intrigues abound in Washington towards the end of the war.

612. Madison, Lucy Foster. A Daughter of the Union. New York: Grosset & Dunlap, 1903.

A young woman carries an important document from New York to Union forces in New Orleans.

613. Magill, Mary Tucker. Women. Baltimore: Turnbull, 1871.

A pro-Southern romance set in Virginia.

614. Magruder, Julia. Across the Chasm. New York: Scribner, 1885.

A love story uniting North and South.

615. Malkus, Alida Sims. We Were There at the Battle of Gettysburg. New York: Grosset & Dunlap, 1955.

A young Gettysburg boy watches the beginning of the great battle and gradually becomes involved in helping the wounded and dying until he is captured by Confederate soldiers.

616. Mally, Emma Louise. Abigail. New York: Appleton, 1956.

A New York abolitionist's marriage to a Southern plantation owner in pre-war Louisville ends in tragedy.

617. ———. The Mockingbird Is Singing. New York: Holt, 1944.

A tangled love story of two couples from New Orleans who move to Texas during the Reconstruction.

618. Malone, Joseph S. Guided and Guarded. New York: Abbey Press, 1901.

Pious incidents in the life of a preacher/ soldier. More religious propaganda than fiction.

619. Marius, Richard. The Coming of Rain. New York: Knopf, 1969.

Memories of the war haunt the inhabitants of an East Tennessee town in a novel one reviewer called "a subdued, poetic romance, a well constructed dream."

620. Markey, Morris. The Band Plays Dixie. New York: Harcourt Brace, 1927.

Two Northern brothers are imprisoned in Richmond, where they both fall in love with the same girl. They escape and stay in the Rebel capital to woo their beloved but they are drafted into the Confederate Army. One dies in a spectacular blaze of glory.

621. Marriott, Crittenden. Sally Castleton, Southerner. Philadelphia: Lippincott, 1913.

A Northern spy sent to Richmond falls in love with a girl who is a Southern spy.

622. Martin, Anne. War Brides. New York: Pegasus, 1940.

A romantic portrait of the Old South and the suffering of war. In the preface the author wrote, "As long as chivalry and courage live, the spirit of the Old South will never die."

623. Martin, Ellen. The Feet of Clay. New York: Brown & Derby, 1882.

Romance and tragedy of a Mississippi family.

624. Martyn, Mrs. Sarah Towne Smith. <u>Our Village</u>
      <u>in War-Time</u>. New York: American Tract
      Society, 1864.

      A religious tract dressed up as a domestic
      novel.

625. Mason, Alfred Bishop. <u>Tom Strong, Lincoln's</u>
      <u>Scout</u>. New York: Holt, 1919.
      Romantic adventures of a Union spy.

626. Mason, Benjamin F. <u>Through War to Peace</u>.
      Oakland: Pacific Publishing Company,
      1891.

      More a recounting of several battles than
      a novel.

627. Mason, Francis Van Wyck. <u>Armoured Giants</u>.
      Boston: Little, Brown, 1980.

      Friends find themselves opposing each
      other on the Monitor and Merrimac.

628. ————. <u>Blue Hurricane</u>. Philadelphia:
      Lippincott, 1954.

      A Maine man's melodramatic activities
      during the River War of 1861-1862 are
      recounted.

629. ————. <u>Hang My Wreath</u>. New York: Funk,
      1941.

      A Rhode Island soldier loves an English
      girl but heads for Antietam.

630. ————. <u>Our Valiant Few</u>. Boston: Little,
      Brown, 1956.

      A robust and rousing tale of Charleston
      and Savannah blockade runners.

631. ————. <u>Proud New Flags</u>. Philadelphia:
      Lippincott, 1951.

      A young man becomes a Confederate hero
      when he builds the Confederate navy.

632. ————. The Trumpets Sound No More.
      Boston: Little, Brown, 1975.

      A Confederate colonel and his company face
      financial and security problems during the
      war's closing days.

633. Masters, Edgar Lee. The Tide of Time.
      New York: Farrar, 1937.

      An Illinois town saga about a liberal
      lawyer, with some Civil War scenes.

634. May, Thomas P. The Earl of Mayfield.
      Philadelphia: T.B. Peterson, 1879.

      A wealthy Louisiana sugar planter is
      opposed to secession but is forced into the
      Confederate forces.

635. McBain, Laurie. When the Splendor Falls.
      New York: Avon, 1985.

      A Confederate horse-breeder's daughter
      loves a Union sympathizer.

636. McCabe, James Dabney, Jr. The Aide de Camp.
      Richmond: W.A.J. Smith, 1863.

      A romance set in Virginia and Maryland.

637. McCord, Joseph. Redhouse On the Hill.
      Philadelphia: Macrae-Smith, 1938.

      A routine romance of a Maryland girl who
      loves a Union Army lieutenant.

638. McElroy, John. The Red Acorn. Chicago:
      Henry A. Sumner, 1883.

      The exploits of the Union Army of the
      Cumberland.

639. ————. Si Klegg, His Transformation from a
      Raw Recruit to a Veteran. Washington:
      National Trubune, 1910.

      The first of a series of novels recounting
      the humorous adventures of some raw recruits
      from Indiana and how they become Union

heroes. The other novels mentioned here are continuations of these adventures.

640. ———. [Si Klegg]; Further Haps and Mishaps to Si Klegg and Shorty. The Second Year of their Service. Washington: National Tribune, 1898.

641. ———. Si Klegg; Si and Shorty Meet Mr. Rosenbaum, the Spy, Who Relates his Adventures. Washington: National Tribune, 1910.

642. ———. Si Klegg: Si and Shorty with their Boy Recruits, Enter on the Atlanta Campaign. Washington: National Tribune, 1915.

643. ———. Si Klegg: Si, Shorty and the Boys are Captured at Kenesaw and Taken to Andersonville. Washington: National Tribune, 1916.

644. ———. Si Klegg: The Deacon's Adventures at Chattanooga in Caring for the Boys. Washington: National Tribune, 1912.

645. ———. Si Klegg Through the Stone River Campaign and in Winter Quarters at Murfreesboro. Washington: National Tribune, 1910.

646. ———. Si, Shorty and the Boys on the March to the Sea. Washington: National Tribune, 1910.

647. McElroy, Lee. Long Way to Texas. New York: Doubleday, 1976.

Some Confederate survivors return home after a defeat.

648. McGehee, Thomasine. Journey Proud. New York: Macmillan, 1939.

A literate and informative look at the passing and decline of the Old South as seen in the declining fortunes of a Virginia family.

649. McGiffin, Lee. A Coat for Private Patrick.
New York: Dutton, 1964.

A young Southerner becomes a telegrapher.

650. ⸺. Rebel Rider. New York: Dutton,
1959.

A Confederate boy scouts for Wade Hampton.

651. McKeen, Phebe Fuller. Theodora. New York:
Randolph, 1875.

The Yankee homefront through the eyes of a
young woman.

652. McLaughlin, N.M. Monroe. The Last Man. New
York: Neale, 1900.

Northern college students volunteer right
after Fort Sumter.

653. McLaws, Emilie Lafayette. The Welding.
Boston: Little, Brown, 1907.

A portrait of an ambitious Georgian in
Washington, DC just before the war and
during the war's early days.

654. McLeod, Isabella. Westfield. Edinburgh:
Edmonston & Douglas, 1866.

How the folks back home in the South
managed to survive.

655. McMahon, Kay. Yankee's Lady. New York:
Zebra, 1986.

A Southern belle finds a Union officer
irresistible.

656. McMeekin, Clark. City of the Flags. New
York: Appleton, 1950.

A wealthy young widow falls in love with a
pro-Confederate medical student, while her
pro-Union father is in trouble with local
secessionists in divided Louisville.

657. ————. <u>Tyrone of Kentucky</u>. New York:
      Appleton, 1954.

      A Confederate soldier returns to his
      Kentucky farm and tries to rebuild it during
      bitter postwar conflict.

658. McNeilly, Mildred Masterson. <u>Praise At</u>
      <u>Morning</u>. New York: Morrow, 1947.

      An arresting novel about a young sea
      captain who helps to bring the Russian fleet
      to American waters in the Northwest - a
      great help to the Union cause.

659. McNicol, Jacqueline Morrell. <u>Ride for Old</u>
      <u>Glory</u>. New York: McKay, 1964.

      A young man serves as aide to Union
      General James Wilson in the 1864 Battle of
      Nashville.

660. Meader, Stephen W. <u>The Muddy Road to</u>
      <u>Glory</u>. New York: Harcourt, 1963.

      A sixteen-year-old farm boy from Maine
      fights in Virginia.

661. ————. <u>Phantom of the Blockade</u>. New York:
      Harcourt, 1962.

      A seventeen-year-old sailor aboard a
      Confederate blockade runner barely escapes
      capture as it plies its way from Bermuda to
      Southern ports.

662. Meadowcroft, Enid LaMonte. <u>By Secret</u>
      <u>Railway</u>. New York: Crowell, 1948.

      A young school dropout gets a job on a
      Chicago waterfront in 1860 and becomes
      enmeshed in Underground Railroad activi-
      ties. A black friend of his is kidnapped
      and taken to Missouri. Vivid and well
      written.

663. Medary, Marjorie. <u>College and Crinoline</u>.
      New York: Longmans, 1937.

A young woman attends college in Iowa where the Northern cause grips the students and local Copperheads are hated.

664. Mellard, Rudolph. Across the Crevasse. New York: Sage, 1966.

Experiences of a Confederate guerilla fighter.

665. Meriwether, Elizabeth Avery. The Sowing of Swords. New York: Neale, 1910.

A Yankee abolitionist's daughter ends up on a Louisiana plantation in a gothic tale steeped in gloom.

666. Miers, Earl S. The Guns of Vicksburg. New York: Putnam, 1957.

A seventeen-year-old Iowan fights at Shiloh and a year later is sent by Grant on a secret mission to Vicksburg.

667. Miller, David. The Red Swan's Neck. Boston: Sherman, French, 1911.

An uneducated North Carolina mountain lad falls in love with a beautiful educated Northern girl. They suffer harrowing experiences during the war but are reunited later.

668. Miller, Edwin J. The Adventures of Ned Minton. Machias, ME: A.R. Furbush, 1904.

A young lad from Maine becomes a Union scout all over Dixie.

669. Miller, Helen Topping. After the Glory. New York: Appleton, 1958.

Two Tennessee brothers who fought on opposite sides are reunited after the war.

670. ————. Christmas for Tad. New York: Longmans, 1956.

Heartwarming incidents occur in the
Lincoln family on one Christmas during the
war.

671. ————. Christmas With Robert E. Lee. New
York: Longmans, 1958.

General Lee tries to rebuild his life that
first Christmas after Appomattox.

672. ————. No Tears for Christmas. New York:
Longmans, 1954.

Union soldiers take over a shattered
Tennessee plantation. The family is in
despair, one son is dead, the other in
hiding. But the Christmas spirit triumphs.
The New York Times said it was "more
lachrymose than literary but many will love
it as a Christmas tale."

673. ————. Rebellion Road. Indianapolis:
Bobbs, Merrill, 1954.

Planters try to rebuild their lives after
Reconstruction.

674. ————. Shod With Flame. Indianapolis:
Bobbs-Merrill, 1946.

Three women love the same Confederate
soldier in Tennessee in 1863. The New York
Times called it "war from the woman's angle
written in quivering-lipped prose."

675. ————. Sing One Song. New York:
Appleton, 1956.

Guerilla raids make Kentucky life
miserable.

676. Miller, May. First the Blade. New York:
Knopf, 1938.

Missouri and California are the locales
for this tale about guerillas and pioneers.

677. Miner, Lewis S. Pilot on the River.
Chicago: Albert Whitman, 1940.

A fifteen-year-old river pilot is placed
in charge of a transport ship.

678. Minnigerode, Meade. Cordelia Chantrell.
     New York: Putnam, 1926.

     The saga of a South Carolina woman who
     loves a Yankee, which Allan Nevins called "a
     harmonious, dramatic and successful romance.

679. Minogue, Anna Catherine. Cardome. New
     York: Collier, 1904.

     A pro-Southern romance set in Kentucky
     during the time of Morgan.

680. Mitchel, Frederick Augustus. Chickamauga.
     New York: Star Book Company, 1892.

     A retelling of the battle.

681. ———. Sweet Revenge. New York: Harper,
     1897.

     A romantic tale of a Tennessee Unionist
     and his daring escapades.

682. Mitchell, Margaret. Gone With the Wind.
     New York: Macmillan, 1936.

     The greatest of them all, this best-seller
     of 1936 and 1937 has sold 25 million copies
     in 27 languages. It has everything.
     Devotees should not miss Gone With the Wind
     as Book and Film (Columbia: University of
     South Carolina Press, 1983), a splendid
     collection of essays edited by Civil War
     specialist Richard Harwell.

683. Mitchell, Silas Weir. A Diplomatic
     Adventure. New York: Macmillan, 1906.

     The U.S. minister to France uncovers a
     pro-Confederate dispatch from the emperor to
     the Queen of England.

684. ———. In War-Time. New York: Houghton
     Mifflin, 1885.

A romance set in Pennsylvania in 1863.

685. ———. <u>Roland Blake</u>. New York: Houghton Mifflin, 1886.

Social life goes on in New York and Philadelphia even though many of its young men are off to war.

686. ———. <u>Westways</u>. New York: Century, 1913.

<u>Booklist</u> called this "a novel of distinction." It is about village life just before the war.

687. Monjo, F.N. <u>The Vicksburg Veteran</u>. New York: Simon & Schuster, 1971.

General Grant's twelve-year-old son accompanies his father through the Vicksburg campaign and narrates this tale.

688. Montgomery, James Stuart. <u>Tall Men</u>. New York: Greenberg, 1927.

An old man looks back and tells of his days as blockade runner for the Confederacy in a novel which is agreeable but has no great depth or reality.

689. Moody, Minnie Hite. <u>Long Meadows</u>. New York: Macmillan, 1941.

Two cousins die in the same battle, fighting for different sides.

690. Moore, Arthur. <u>Look Down, Look Down</u>. New York: Powell, 1970.

A madman leads untrained Southern recruits against an experienced Yankee regiment.

691. Moore, Virginia. <u>Rising Wind</u>. New York: Dutton, 1928.

A Southern girl feels she must choose between father and lover in a novel which

reviewers called sentimental, unreal and
unconvincing.

692. Mordecai, Alfred. The Uncommon Soldier.
New York: Farrar, 1959.

693. Morford, Henry. The Coward. Philadelphia:
T.B. Peterson, 1864.

694. ————. The Days of Shoddy. Philadelphia:
T.B. Peterson, 1863.

695. ————. Shoulder Straps. Philadelphia:
T.B. Peterson, 1863.

All three of Morford's novels consist of
social and economic criticism of corruption
and war profiteering in the North.

696. Morgan, George. The Issue. Philadelphia:
Lippincott, 1904.

Antietam, Chancellorsville, and Charleston
figure in this novel.

697. Morrill, Mrs. Lily Logan. Virginia's War.
Philadelphia: Dorrance, 1935.

A romance with a nice Christmas setting.

698. Morris, Anthony P. Old Fusee; or The
Cannon's Last Shot. New York: Novelist
Publishing Company, 1883.

Battle of Antietam.

699. Morris, Gouverneur. Aladdin O'Brien. New
York: Century, 1902.

A Yankee hero's tale.

700. Morrison, Gerry. Unvexed to the Sea. New
York: St. Martins, 1961.

A novel which concentrates on the military
(siege of Vicksburg and Sherman's March)
also includes soap opera romances. Library
Journal called it "memorably dull."

701. Morrow, Decatur Franklin. <u>Then and Now,</u>
<u>Reminiscenses and Historical Romance,</u>
<u>1856-1865.</u> Macon, GA: J.W. Burke, 1926.

In Rutherford County, North Carolina the
home guard are waiting for a massive slave
uprising on December 13, 1863.

702. Morrow, Honore Willsie. <u>Forever Free</u>. New
York: Morrow, 1927.

An attractive Southern woman in Lincoln's
household is really a spy.

703. ————. <u>The Last Full Measure</u>. New York:
Morrow, 1930.

Lincoln's last few months.

704. ————. <u>With Malice Toward None</u>. New York:
Morrow, 1928.

This novel concentrates on the last two
years of the war and Lincoln's conflict with
Sumner. Mrs. Lincoln plays a major part.
In 1935 Morrow published all three of the
above novels in an omnibus volume entitled
<u>Great Captain</u>.

705. Murfree, Mary. <u>The Storm Centre</u>. New York:
Grosset & Dunlap, 1905.

Union soldiers court local girls in the
mountains of Tennessee in a novel one
reviewer called "slight in substance and of
moderate interest."

706. ————. <u>Where the Battle Was Fought</u>.
Boston: Houghton, Mifflin, 1884.

A standard wartime romance.

707. Musick, John R. <u>Brother Against Brother</u>.
New York: J.S. Ogilvie, 1887.

A long drawn out retelling of the whole
war, which he continued in the sequel,
<u>Union</u>.

708. ———. Union. New York: Funk & Wagnalls,
      1894.

709. Nelson, Truman John. The Surveyor. New
      York: Doubleday, 1960.

      "Bleeding Kansas," the battle between
      pro-slavery and anti-slavery forces just
      before the war.

710. Newbrough, J.B. The Fall of Fort Sumter; or
      Love and War in 1860-1861. New York:
      Brady, 1867.

      A silly romance.

711. Nichols, George Ward. The Sanctuary. New
      York: Harper, 1866.

      All about Sherman's march to the sea by an
      author who served on Sherman's staff.

712. Noble, Hollister. Woman With a Sword. New
      York: Doubleday, 1948.

      A fictional biography of Anna Carroll, a
      Maryland woman who advised Lincoln on
      military strategy. Reprinted as The Winds
      of Love (New York: Kensington, 1977)

713. Nolan, Jeannette C. Belle Boyd, Secret
      Agent. New York: Messner, 1967.

      A gentle Maryland woman becomes a daring
      spy for the South in this novel based on
      fact.

714. ———. Spy for the Confederacy: Rose
      O'Neal Greenhow. New York: Messner,
      1960.

      A biographical novel of another Maryland
      woman who spied for the South.

715. Norris, Mary Harriott. The Grapes of
      Wrath. Boston: Small, Maynard, 1901.

      A Virginia family suffers as the war comes
      to an end.

716. Norton, Alice Mary. Rebel Spurs. New York: World, 1962.

     A novel set in postwar Arizona.

717. ————. Ride Proud, Rebel. New York: World, 1961.

     A young scout in Morgan's Raiders becomes disillusioned as the hopelessness of the Southern cause becomes evident.

Norton, Andre. See Norton, Alice Mary

718. Norton, Charles Ledyard. Jack Benson's Log. Boston: W.A. Wilde, 1895.

     Recollections of a Union sailor.

719. ————. A Medal of Honor Man. Boston: W.A. Wilde, 1896.

     Blockade runners in Florida cause the Union trouble.

720. O'Connor, Florence J. The Heroine of the Confederacy. London: Harrison, 1865.

     A long, involved saga of a Louisiana sugar plantation.

721. O'Connor, Richard. Company Q. New York: Doubleday, 1957.

     Union men who had been demoted or disciplined struggle to regain honor and respect.

722. ————. The Guns of Chickamauga. New York: Doubleday, 1955.

     A young Chicago reporter is cashiered from the Union army in a standard adventure-romance.

723. O'Dell, Scott. The 290. Boston: Houghton Mifflin, 1976.

A British boy, an apprentice at a shipyard in Liverpool, works on a ship which becomes the <u>Alabama</u>, the great Confederate cruiser. He decides to ship aboard and becomes involved in the war.

724. Odum, John D. <u>Hell in Georgia</u>. New York: Corlies Macy, 1960.

Sherman's march, what else.

725. Oldham, Henry. <u>The Man from Texas</u>. New York: Petersen, 1884.

The exploits of a Confederate guerilla chief.

726. Olsen, Theodore V. <u>There Was a Season</u>. New York: Doubleday, 1972.

A biographical novel of Jefferson Davis.

727. O'Neal, Cothburn. <u>Untold Glory</u>. New York: Crown, 1957.

A Tennessee woman befriends Union officers in order to smuggle desperately needed medical supplies into Memphis.

Optic, Oliver. See Adams, William T.

728. Orpen, Adela E. <u>The Jay-Hawkers</u>. New York: Appleton, 1900.

"Bleeding Kansas" in all its misery.

Otis, James. See Kaler, James O.

729. Page, Thomas Nelson. <u>A Captured Santa Claus</u>. New York: Scribner, 1902.

A charming, sentimental Christmas story about the son of a Southern colonel who helps his father gain an extended parole from the war.

730. ———. <u>Gordon Keith</u>. New York: Scribner, 1903.

The son of a Virginia gentleman is a victim of the war but his chivalric code sustains him when he moves to New York. Reviewers called it lengthy, ambitious and disorganized but the public loved it.

731. ————. Meh Lady. New York: Scribner, 1893.

An archetypal story of reconciliation between North and South, accomplished by a marriage of a Northern man and a Southern lady. Noted for pathos and sentimentality.

732. ————. The Red Riders. New York: Scribner, 1924.

In Reconstruction South Carolina disgruntled whites establish a "defensive brigade" to fight excesses. The old Southern way of life triumphs completely.

733. ————. Red Rock. New York: Scribner, 1899.

Regional reconciliation through the capitulation of Yankees to Southern values is the theme of this Reconstruction novel. It is considered to be the most effective Southern refutation of Uncle Tom's Cabin.

734. ————. Two Little Confederates. New York: Scribner, 1888.

The war as seen through two young boys on a Virginia plantation. Page's biographer, Theodore Gross, called it "a kind of Virginian Tom Sawyer without the relief of Mark Twain's humor." Page was a supreme interpreter of antebellum Southern life whose Civil War novels were popular in both regions. Literary critic, Edmund Wilson, once wrote, "It was hard to make the Civil War seem cozy but Thomas Nelson Page did his best."

735. Palmer, Bruce. Many Are the Hearts. New York: Simon & Schuster, 1961.

Four stories form a kind of novel about valour.

736. Palmer, Frederick. <u>The Vagabond</u>. New York: Scribner, 1903.

Romance and war in Virginia.

737. Parkings, W.H. <u>How I Escaped</u>. New York: Home Publishing Company, 1889.

A trite tale of a Union soldier who had to fight to win his love.

738. Parrish, Anne. <u>A Clouded Star</u>. New York: Harper, 1948.

The story of Harriet Tubman and the Underground Railroad, which the <u>New York Herald Tribune</u> called "a little masterpiece."

739. Parrish, Randall. <u>Love Under Fire</u>. Chicago: McClurg, 1911.

A typical romance between a Northern man and a Southern woman.

740. ————. <u>My Lady of the North</u>. Chicago: McClurg, 1904.

The adventures of a courier for General Lee in the Shenandoah.

741. ————. <u>My Lady of the South</u>. Chicago: McClurg, 1909.

A bitter feud between two Southern families endures despite war. A gallant Union officer wins his Southern belle.

742. ————. <u>The Red Mist</u>. Chicago: McClurg, 1914.

A young Confederate officer is sent to West Virginia to investigate the strength of Union support. Under a disguised name, he encounters a girl he had known in childhood.

743. Paterson, Arthur. The Gospel Writ in
     Steel. New York: Appleton, 1898.

     The Wisconsin role in the Union army.

744. Pease, Verne Seth. In the Wake of War.
     Chicago: George M. Hill, 1900.

     A tale of the South under the carpet-
     baggers.

745. [Peck, Ellen]. Renshawe. New York:
     Carleton, 1867.

     The saga of a female spy.

746. [Peck, George W.]. How Private George W.
     Peck Put Down the Rebellion. Chicago:
     Belford, Clarke, 1887.

     The humorous, first-person account of a
     raw recruit.

747. Peck, William Henry. The McDonalds.
     New York: Metropolitan Record Office,
     1867.

     Immortalizing Southern women, this is a
     tale of Sherman's march through Georgia,
     leaving Southern homes in ashes. The hero
     is a Georgia lady whose husband and five
     sons all perish.

748. Pendleton, Louis Beauregard. Echo of Drums.
     New York: Sovereign House, 1938.

     Georgia plantation life after the war.

749. ————. In the Okefenokee. Boston:
     Roberts, 1895.

     Two inquisitive boys living in the south
     Georgia swamps observe deserters and
     prisoners hiding out from authorities. This
     charming homefront novel has a lyrical-
     pastoral quality.

750. Pennell, Joseph Stanley. <u>The History of
     Rome Hanks and Kindred Matters</u>. New York:
     Scribner, 1944.

     In this now classic novel, a man searches
     his family history and finds his grandfather
     and great grandfather were illustrious Civil
     War fighters. Reviewers raved, comparing it
     to Thomas Wolfe. The <u>Yale Review</u> labeled it
     "brilliant, powerful, perplexing, irritat-
     ing." It has an obscure, racy, and ribald
     style.

751. Penney, Kate Mayhew Speake. <u>Cross Currents</u>.
     Boston: Bruce Humphries, 1938.

     An Ohio schoolteacher marries a Southern
     gentleman and learns to understand the
     South's traditions.

752. Peple, Edward. <u>The Littlest Rebel</u>. New
     York: Moffat, Yard, 1911.

     A sentimental novella of an old plantation
     twenty miles south of Richmond. Union
     soldiers arrive looking for a little girl's
     father, who is a Confederate spy. She wins
     them with her charm.

753. Perenyi, Eleanor. <u>The Bright Sword</u>. New
     York: Rinehart, 1955.

     A sketch of General John Bell Hood and his
     love affair with a beautiful aristocrat.

754. Pickett, La Salle Corbell. <u>The Bugles of
     Gettysburg</u>. Chicago: F.G. Browne, 1913.

     A fair-minded novel written by the wife of
     Confederate General Pickett on the 50th
     anniversary of the Battle of Gettysburg.

755. Pierce, Ovid Williams. <u>The Devil's Half</u>.
     New York: Doubleday, 1968.

     A strong-willed Southern woman is
     determined to preserve a way of life on her
     plantation after the war.

756. ────. <u>On a Lonesome Porch</u>. New York:
      Doubleday, 1960.

The remaining members of a North Carolina
family return to their shattered home to try
to rebuild their lives after the war.
<u>Booklist</u> said it "conveys the spirit of a
South still stunned by the havoc of a Civil
War, while the <u>New York Herald Tribune</u> said
it "has the economy and grace of a Chinese
watercolor."

757. Place, Marian T. <u>Steamboat Up the Missouri</u>.
      New York: Viking, 1958.

A sixteen-year-old pilot helps the Union
army on a dangerous mission.

758. Plain, Belva. <u>Crescent City</u>. New York:
      Delacorte, 1984.

Brought by her father from Germany to New
Orleans, a Jewish woman struggles to
reconcile her life as a Southern wife and
mother with her passion for a forbidden man
and a forbidden cause (the Union).

759. Plum, William R. <u>The Sword and the Soul</u>.
      New York: Neale, 1917.

A romance.

760. Prescott, John. <u>Valley of Wrath</u>. New York:
      Fawcett, 1961.

A handful of Yankees battle Indians and
rebels in the Southwest.

761. Price, Anthony. <u>Sion Crossing</u>. New York:
      Mysterious Press, 1985.

A contemporary spy novel, with intriguing
references to Sherman's March.

762. Price, Eugenia. <u>Margaret's Story</u>. New
      York: Lippincott & Crowell, 1980.

This final novel of the author's Florida
trilogy includes much more than the Civil

War but it does show the drastic change in personal fortunes of a Florida plantation owner. Her St. John's River home became a notable tourist lodging for Northern visitors after the war.

763. Putnam, George I. _In Blue Uniform_. New York: Scribner, 1893.

This novel and its sequel are stories of a Union brigade called the Old Regiment.

764. ————. _On the Offensive_. New York: Scribner, 1894.

765. [Queen, Sister Mary Xavier]. _Elise_. Boston: Angel Guardian Press, 1896.

Pious story about a young child's life on a New Orleans plantation during the war.

766. Quick, Herbert. _Vandermark's Folly_. Indianapolis: Bobbs-Merrill, 1922.

The romantic adventures of a Dutch farmer in prewar Iowa.

767. Raine, William MacLeod. _Arkansas Guns_. Boston: Houghton, Mifflin, 1954.

Planters have a tough time during Reconstruction.

768. Rand, Edward A. _The Drummer Boy of the Rappahannock_. New York: Hunt & Eaton, 1889.

Adventures of a very young fellow.

769. Rauch, Mabel Thompson. _Vinnie and the Flag Tree_. New York: Duell, 1959.

The war's effect on life in southern Illinois.

770. Read, Opie Percival and Frank Pixley. _The Carpetbagger_. Chicago: Laird & Lee, 1899.

A novelized version of a popular play satirizing Reconstruction days.

771.   Redgate, John. <u>Barlow's Kingdom</u>. New York: Simon & Schuster, 1969.

A Civil War veterans begin a new life in Montana.

772.   Reed, Ishmael. <u>Flight to Canada</u>. New York: Random House, 1976.

A slave escapes to Canada in a fantastic comedy which <u>Saturday Review</u> called, "a brilliant, outrageous spoof."

773.   Reese, Lizette Woodworth. <u>Worleys</u>. New York: Farrar, 1936.

A nostalgic portrait of a Civil War childhood by a Maryland poet. The novella begins as Lee surrenders and a girl wonders if her officer father will ever come home.

774.   [Reeves, Marion Calhoon and Legare]. <u>Randolph Honor</u>. New York: Richardson, 1868.

Romance and fighting in an "ivied mansion of the good old times."

Reid, Christian. See Tiernan, Mary

Reising, Otto. See Strohl, Paul

775.   Remick, Martha. <u>Millicent Halford</u>. Boston: Williams, 1865.

A New England orphan girl living in northern Kentucky in 1861 witnesses the tragegy of civil strife and becomes engaged to a Union officer.

776.   Reno, Marie R. <u>When the Music Changed</u>. New York: New American Library, 1980.

An independent-minded woman is loved by three men in the New York of 1860. Then the guns roared and the war that changed America forever changed them, too.

777. Rhodes, James A. and Dean Jauchius. Johnny
      Shiloh. Indianapolis: Bobbs-Merrill,
      1959.

      A novel based on a true story about the
      war's youngest soldier.

778. Richardson, Norval. The Heart of Hope.
      New York: Dodd, Mead, 1905.

      An uncommonly interesting sentimental
      romance about the siege of Vicksburg and
      General Grant.

779. Roark, Garland. The Outlawed Banner. New
      York: Doubleday, 1956.

      A U.S. Army officer falls in love with a
      Southern girl during a visit to an Alabama
      plantation. Her brother becomes a
      Confederate naval officer.

780. Roberts, Eldridge Gerry. A Naval
      Engagement. Redbank, NJ: Privately
      Printed, 1918.

      An American living in Scotland hurries
      home to fight for the Union and becomes an
      engineer on a Union gunboat.

781. Roberts, MacLennan. The Great Locomotive
      Chase. New York: Dell, 1956.

      A Union spy and an ex-house painter lead
      the attack on a Southern supply train. A
      harrowing 87-mile chase follows.

782. Roberts, Maggie. Home Scenes During the
      Rebellion. New York: John F. Trow,
      1875.

      An asinine "first" novel about the
      triumphs of love, written by an individual
      who had absolutely no talent for writing.

783. Roberts, Walter Adolphe. Brave Mardi Gras.
      Indianapolis: Bobbs-Merrill, 1946.

A Louisiana soldier fights at Bull Run and in Texas. Filled with love, romance and spies. The author was a Jamaican who became an ardent partisan of the Lost Cause.

784. Robertson, Constance. <u>Firebell in the Night</u>. New York: Holt, 1944.

The Underground Railroad in Syracuse is a beehive of activity just before the war.

785. ————. <u>The Golden Circle</u>. New York: Random House, 1951.

An excellent novel which recreates the atmosphere of divided Ohio, concentrating on Copperhead sentiment.

786. ————. <u>Salute To the Hero</u>. New York: Farrar, 1942.

A character study of an evil man who prospered during the war and after. Probably based on Daniel Sickles, this novel is "admirably constructed, soundly executed and thoroughly finished in both characterization and event."

787. ————. <u>The Unterrified</u>. New York: Henry Holt, 1946.

In upstate New York Senator King, a Peace Democrat, and his Southern wife fight for an early peace and urge cease fire. She influences her stepsons to oppose the draft.

788. Robertson, Don. <u>By Antietam Creek</u>. Englewood Cliffs: Prentice-Hall, 1960.

A moment by moment reconstruction of the bloody battle. <u>Kirkus</u> thought it was "rambling if well researched."

789. ————. <u>The River and the Wilderness</u>. New York: Doubleday, 1962.

Concentrates on Burnside at Fredericksburg and the Wilderness Campaign, though it contains several lurid love stories. The

New York Herald Tribune thought it was
"overlong and overwritten but powerful and
gutsy," but the Chicago Tribune called it
"an exercise in vulgarity."

790.   ————. The Three Days. Englewood Cliffs:
        Prentice-Hall, 1959.

        The battle of Gettysburg seen through the
        private lives of a few soldiers. Most
        reviewers thought it was impressive,
        convincing and often moving.

791.   Robins, Edwards. Chasing an Iron Horse.
        Philadelphia: George W. Jacobs, 1902.

        A young man joins Andrews' Raiders.

792.   ————. With Thomas in Tennessee.
        Philadelphia: George W. Jacobs, 1903.

        A young man serves as an aide to General
        George Thomas.

793.   Robinson, Benjamin. Dolores. New York:
        E.J. Hale, 1868.

        The tribulations of a North Carolina
        family include a murder trial.

794.   Robinson, Edward A., and George A. Wall. The
        Gun-Bearer. New York: Robert Bonner,
        1894.

        A vivid account of a young Union recruit
        who fights at Nashville and Franklin. Gives
        excellent insight into the daily life of the
        average soldier.

795.   Robinson, Mary Stephenson. The Brother
        Soldiers. New York: N. Tibbals, 1866.

        A didactic pro-Union account.

796.   Roe, Edward Payson. The Earth Trembled.
        New York: Dodd, Mead, 1887.

        Saga of a South Carolina family.

797.   ————. His Sombre Rivals. New York:
        Dodd, Mead, 1883.

        Romance centered on the Battle of Bull
        Run.

798.   ————. Miss Lou. New York: Dodd, Mead,
        1888.

799.   ————. An Original Belle. New York:
        Dodd, Mead, 1885.

800.   Roe, Edward Reynolds. The Gray and the
        Blue. Chicago: Rand McNally, 1884.

        A tale of sectional reconciliation through
        love.

801.   Roe, Louis A. The Battle of the Ironclads.
        New York: Cupples & Leon, 1942.

        A young officer is given command of the
        Monitor, a strange new ironclad about which
        his fellow officers are skeptical.

802.   Rose, George Hamlin. Beyond the River.
        Boston: Meador, 1938.

        A poorly written romance of the Border
        States.

803.   Rowell, Adelaide Corinne. On Jordan's
        Stormy Banks. Indianapolis: Bobbs-
        Merrill, 1948.

        The life of Sam Davis, Confederate scout
        who was hanged at the age of twenty one.

804.   Royce, George M. The Little Bugler. St.
        Louis: G.J. Jones, 1880.

        A fifteen-year-old boy observes war in
        Kentucky and decides to join. His brother,
        a West Point graduate, dies for the Union.

805.   Rumbough, George P.C. From Dust to Ashes.
        Little Rock: Brown Printing Co., 1895.

Valiant troops from the Virginia Military Academy fight for hearth and home.

806. Runkel, William M. <u>Wontus</u>. Philadelphia: Lippincott, 1874.

Semi-humorous account of a pompous man who goes off to war.

807. Russell, Charles Wells. <u>Roebuck</u>. New York: M. Doolady, 1866.

Yet another plantation saga.

808. Rutledge, Archibald Hamilton. <u>My Colonel and His Lady</u>. Indianapolis: Bobbs, Merrill, 1937.

Plantation life on the Santee River in South Carolina.

809. Ryals, J.V. <u>Yankee Doodle Dixie</u>. Richmond: Everett Waddey, 1890.

Many Virginians love both the Union and their native state.

810. Sage, William. <u>The Claybornes</u>. Boston: Houghton Mifflin, 1902.

All about Grant at Vicksburg and Richmond.

811. Sargent, Epes. <u>Peculiar</u>. New York: Carleton, 1864.

A pro-Northern novel depicting blacks as noble.

812. Sass, Herbert Ravenel. <u>Look Back to Glory</u>. Indianapolis: Bobbs-Merrill, 1933.

A retired diplomat realizes that the old order is doomed and that secession will destroy the South. Yet he dies defending Fort Sumter. <u>Books and Bookmen</u> said this novel "paid tribute to the bright beauty of a departed age but did not ignore its social imperfections." <u>The New York Times</u> thought it was a "richly readable and satisfying"

account of the glamorous life of Tidewater
South Carolina.

813. Savage, Richard Henry. In the House of His
Friends. New York: Home Publishing Co.,
1901.

A history of the war with a plethora of
characters.

814. Sawyer, Susan Fontaine. The Priestess of
the Hills. Boston: Meador, 1928.

Blacks and whites get along just fine on a
Mississippi plantation.

815. Sayre, Anne. Never Call Retreat. New York:
Crowell, 1953.

A Quaker family's experiences in postwar
Alabama.

816. Schachner, Nathan. By the Dim Lamps. New
York: Stokes, 1941.

A lively account of New Orleans life
during war and Reconstruction.

817. Schaefer, Jack W. Company of Cowards.
Boston: Houghton Mifflin, 1957.

A group of Yankee cowards and renegades
who broke and ran under pressure prove their
bravery after being given a second chance.

818. Schuster, Richard. The Selfish and the
Strong. New York: Random House, 1958.

A common law wife in a small Kentucky town
tries to protect what little she has against
both sides.

819. Scott, Evelyn. The Wave. New York:
Jonathan Cape, 1929.

Richard Harwell said, "It is a remarkably
good novel and set a new standard for
fictional treatment of the war. Mrs. Scott
gave the Civil War novel a depth that, with

few exceptions, it had previously
lacked...."

820. Scott, George. <u>Tamarack Farm</u>. New York:
Grafton, 1903.

Based on the true story of Jennie Wade,
who died at Gettysburg while taking water to
soldiers.

821. Scott, Lucy Jameson. <u>The Gilead Guards</u>.
New York: Hunt & Eaton, 1891.

A New England town is changed by the war.

822. Seabrook, Phoebe Hamilton. <u>A Daughter of
the Confederacy</u>. New York: Neale, 1906.

A glimpse of domestic life in Dixie.

923. Seawell, Molly Elliott. <u>Throckmorton</u>. New
York: Appleton, 1890.

A tale of Reconstruction Virginia.

824. ————. <u>The Victory</u>. New York: Appleton,
1906.

The adopted daughter of a Virginia family
marries the son who supports the Union.
While he is at war she falls in love with a
Frenchman. She remains faithful but her
husband dies in battle.

825. Sedger, John. <u>The Angry Wife</u>. New York:
John Day, 1947.

Two brothers who fought on different sides
come home to rebuild their lives.

826. Seifert, Shirley. <u>Farewell My General</u>.
Philadelphia: Lippincott, 1954.

The life of Jeb Stuart from courtship to
death.

827. ————. <u>Look to the Rose</u>. Philadelphia:
Lippincott, 1960.

The romance of a Northern girl who marries a Southerner and lives in Georgia before, during and after the war.

828. ————. The Wayfarer. New York: M.S.
Mill, 1938.

The life and loves of a New Yorker who drifts from whaling to cattle breeding with a bit of Civil War background.

829. Selph, Fannie Eoline. Texas. West
Nashville, TN: Privately Printed, 1905.

A pro-Southern romance about the siege of Vicksburg. The heroine is a woman from Galveston.

830. Settle, Mary Lee. Know Nothing. New York:
Viking, 1960.

Life on a western Virginia plantation just before the war.

831. Shaara, Michael. The Killer Angels. New
York: McKay, 1974.

A Pulitzer Prize-winning reconstruction of the Battle of Gettysburg.

832. Shannon, Doris. Cain's Daughter. New York:
St. Martin's, 1978.

A Northern industrialist's daughter marries a wealthy Georgian and flees with him to England, where he attempts to enlist support for the Southern cause. She is disowned by her family, yet distrusted by his. They return to his Georgia plantation just before Sherman arrives.

833. Shaw, Linda. Ballad in Blue. New York:
Ballantine, 1979.

A Southern widow marries a Union soldier, whom she does not love, in order to give her son a decent life. Moving to his Maryland home after the war she gradually falls in

love with him and awaits the birth of their
first child.

834. Sheehy, Julia Williams. William Winston.
      New York: Broadway Publishing, 1913.

      A romance of old Virginia emphasizing
      patriotism and courage.

835. Shelton, William Henry. The Last Three
      Soldiers. New York: Century, 1897.

      Three Union soldiers are lost somewhere in
      the Southern mountains late in the war.

836. Sherburne, James. The Way to Fort Pillow.
      Boston: Houghton Mifflin, 1972.

      A Kentucky boy leaves Berea College and
      joins the Union Army, even though his
      brother fights for the Confederacy. He
      joins an all-black unit and survives the
      Fort Pillow Massacre. Library Journal said:
      "An historical novel of the first order,
      this combines the politics, plots and
      counterplots of Civil War Washington and a
      tender love story."

837. Shields, S.J. A Chevalier of Dixie. New
      York: Neale, 1907.

      A Mississippi lawyer recalls his service
      to the Lost Cause, telling about a polished
      gentle hero who becomes a man during the
      war and returns two years later after his
      family thought him dead.

838. Shirreffs, Gordon D. The Border Guidon.
      New York: New American Library, 1962.

      A Union soldier rides through Apache-held
      Oklahoma to rescue his captain's daughter
      and to prevent arms from reaching the
      Confederacy.

839. ———. The Mosquito Fleet. Philadelphia:
      Chilton, 1961.

The misadventures of two Yankee boys in
Mississippi. After numerous adventures they
find themselves fighting on the wrong side
at Vicksburg.

840.   ———.   Roanoke Raiders.   Philadelphia:
        Westminster, 1959.

A pro-Union North Carolina boy helps
destroy a Confederate ship in Albemarle
Sound.

841.   Shuster, George Nauman.   Look Away.   New
        York: Macmillan, 1939.

A Southern lawyer in Wisconsin is torn
between love for his Northern wife and
devotion to the Confederate cause.   She
struggles to keep her home, pride and love
in a hostile environment while he is at war.

842.   Simons, Katherine.   The Running Thread.   New
        York: Appleton, 1949.

An Irish girl falls in love with a
Charleston man and remains faithful to him
during the hard years of the war.

843.   Sims, Marian.   Beyond Surrender.
        Philadelphia: Lippincott, 1942.

In Reconstruction South Carolina a return-
ing Confederate army major takes over the
family plantation and becomes politically
influential.

844.   Sinclair, Harold Augustus.   The Horse
        Soldiers.   New York: Harper, 1956.

The New York Times called this reconstruction of Grierson's Raid "a well
conceived, masterly written novel of men,
guts and guns."

845.   ———.   The Years of Growth: 1861-1893.
        New York: Doubleday, 1940.

A plain, unadorned tale of an Illinois
town during wartime and the postwar years.

846. Sinclair, Upton. <u>Manassas</u>. New York:
     Macmillan, 1904.

     Heavy into battle scenes, a military-
     oriented novel.

847. Singmaster, Elsie. <u>A Boy at Gettysburg</u>.
     Boston: Houghton Mifflin, 1924.

     A young lad aids Union soldiers.

848. ————. <u>Emmeline</u>. Boston: Houghton
     Mifflin, 1916.

     A fifteen-year-old girl is sent to her
     grandfather's farm and soldiers appear on
     the streets of Gettysburg. She discovers
     reality of war and learns compassion for the
     enemy troops.

849. ————. <u>Gettysburg</u>. Boston: Houghton
     Mifflin, 1913.

850. ————. <u>The Loving Heart</u>. Boston:
     Houghton Mifflin, 1937.

     A girl of nineteen shows heroism and self-
     sacrifice during the Gettysburg battle. Her
     grandmother, with whom she lives, works
     secretly for the Underground Railroad.

851. ————. <u>Swords of Steel</u>. Boston: Houghton
     Mifflin, 1933.

     A fourteen-year-old Gettysburg boy
     observes the war and then enlists.

852. Slaughter, Frank Gill. <u>In a Dark Garden</u>.
     New York: Doubleday, 1946.

     A young Confederate surgeon helps save
     lives on both sides. He fights for better
     medical care and marries a beautiful Union
     spy. Set in St. Augustine, Florida.

853. ————. <u>Lorena</u>. New York: Doubleday, 1959.

A doctor becomes enmeshed in Sherman's March.

854. ———. The Passionate Rebel. New York: Doubleday, 1979.

A countess arrives in Mobile to observe the war but becomes so embroiled in the conflict that she becomes a spy for the Confederacy.

855. ———. The Stonewall Brigade. New York: Doubleday, 1975.

A surgeon accompanies Stonewall Jackson in the Shenandoah Valley Campaign.

856. ———. Storm Haven. New York: Doubleday, 1953.

A Texas doctor rescues a beautiful woman from her husband during a Florida cattle drive.

857. ———. The Stubborn Heart. New York: Doubleday, 1950.

A doctor's wife converts a plantation into a hospital after the war ends in a novel The New York Times labeled "high-grade, medico-historical fiction."

858. Slotkin, Richard. The Crater. New York: Atheneum, 1980.

A fictional retelling of the disastrous Battle of the Crater in Petersburg, Virginia on July 30, 1864. Coal miners from Pennsylvania devise a plan to tunnel under Rebel trenches and blow a hole in fortifications. A black regiment of ex-slaves plays a key role.

859. Smith, Chard Powers. Artillery of Time. New York: Scribner, 1939.

An impressive, penetrating and distinguished recreation of Upstate New York life before and during the war.

860. Smith, Francis Hopkinson. The Fortunes of
      Oliver Horn. New York: Scribner, 1902.

      Artistic life in New York survives the
      war.

861. Smith, George C. The Boy in Gray. Macon:
      Macon Publishing, 1894.

      The saga of a very religious Georgia
      family, which includes a North-South
      marriage as a symbol of reconciliation.

862. Smith, William Ferguson. The Rival Lovers.
      Atlanta: Peachtree Publishers, 1980.

      A sixteen-year-old Georgia boy goes to do
      battle for the doomed Confederacy. He
      returns from battle and from prison with a
      great sadness but no malice in his heart and
      sets out to win his love against a rival
      suitor. This novel was originally
      serialized in a Butts County, Georgia
      newspaper in 1877 but was not published in
      book form for another century until his
      great granddaughter discovered the yellowed
      newspaper clippings.

863. Sobol, Donald J. The Lost Dispatch, A Story
      of Antietam. New York: Watts, 1958.

      A tense and colorful story of a sargeant
      of the Kentucky Volunteers who bears an
      uncanny resemblance to a Confederate
      soldier, for whom he is mistaken on a spy
      mission to Tennessee. He rejoins his Union
      comrades and plays a decisive role at
      Antietam. Very well written.

864. Sosey, Frank H. Robert Devoy. Palmyra, MO:
      Sosey Bros., 1903.

      Ten Confederate prisoners are shot by
      Union troops in Marion County, Missouri one
      October day in 1862.

865. Spencer, Bella Z. Tried and True.
      Springfield, MA: W.T. Holland, 1866.

A woman wed to an Alabama slave owner
finds happiness with a Union officer she
nurses in a Paducah hospital.

866. Spooner, Arthur Willis. Pauline. Boston:
      Sherman French, 1915.

      A tender Victorian romance of a pure New
      Jersey girl who impulsively kisses an
      unknown soldier goodbye one day in 1861 at
      the Jersey City railroad station. Not even
      knowing each other's names, they remain true
      to the memory and are miraculously reunited
      after the war. They are married seven years
      to the day of the first kiss and he becomes
      a Presbyterian minister.

867. Stables, William Gordon. For Life and
      Liberty. London: Blackie, 1896.

      A Virginia family saga.

868. ————. Sweeping the Seas. New York:
      Dutton, 1902.

      A tale of the Confederate ship Alabama.
      The author was a surgeon in the royal navy.

869. Stacton, David. The Judges of the Secret
      Court. New York: Pantheon, 1961.

      A psychological study of John Wilkes
      Booth's last twelve days.

870. Stanley, Caroline Abbott. Order No. 11.
      New York: Century, 1904.

      A tale of Union Confederate strife in
      Missouri.

871. Statham, Frances Patton. Flame of New
      Orleans. New York: Gold Medal, 1977.

      A bold and beauteous Confederate spy falls
      in love with a Union officer who saves her
      life and then forces her into an unusual
      marriage.

872. Steele, William. The Perilous Road. New
      York: Harcourt, 1958.

A Tennessee mountain boy aids the South but his older brother joins the Union.

873. Steelman, Robert J. The Galvanized Rebel. New York: Doubleday, 1977.

The Confederates try to stir up the Plains Indians against the Union.

874. Stephenson, Nathaniel. They That Took the Sword. New York: John Lane, 1901.

A romantic spy story set in Cincinnati.

875. Sterling, Dorothy. Freedom Train. New York: Doubleday, 1954.

A sympathetic portrait of Harriet Tubman.

876. Stern, Phillip Van Doren. The Drums of Morning. New York: Doubleday, 1942.

The son of an abolitionist from Illinois fights for the Union. This pro-Northern novel contrasting innocent Yankee males with promiscuous Southern rich women was briefly on the bestseller lists.

877. ————. The Man Who Killed Lincoln. New York: Random House, 1939.

A biography of Booth in semi-fictional form.

878. Sterne, Emma Gelders. No Surrender. New York: Duffield, 1932.

A tenacious Alabama woman tries to keep her dying plantation alive with the help of her twelve-year-old son and two faithful blacks.

879. Stevenson, Janet. Weep No More. New York: Viking, 1957.

The story of "Crazy Bet," a Richmond lady who opposed slavery and secession and spied for the Union.

880. Steward, Davenport. Sail the Dark Tide.
    Atlanta: Tupper & Love, 1954.

    A U.S. Navy lieutenant resigns his
    commission and returns to his native state
    of North Carolina to become a blockade
    runner between Wilmington and Nassau.

881. Stewart, Catherine. Three Roads to
    Valhalla. New York: Scribners, 1948.

    A Yankee girl goes to Jacksonville,
    Florida after the war with her father who
    heads the hated freedman's bureau. He is
    murdered and she marries a scoundrel in this
    readable, well-told tale.

882. Stewart, Fred Mustard. A Rage Against
    Heaven. New York: Viking, 1978.

    An interlocking novel about America, Paris
    and Mexico in the 1860s.

883. Stoddard, William O. The Battle of New
    York. New York: Appleton, 1892.

    Spies and draft riots harm the Union cause
    in New York.

884. ————. Long Bridge Boys. Boston: Lothrop,
    1904.

    Espionage activity in Washington, D.C. and
    Virginia.

885. Stover, Herbert Elisha. Copperhead Moon.
    New York: Dodd, Mead, 1952.

    Union deserters and Copperheads try to
    sabotage the Union war effort in Pennsyl-
    vania but fail in a novel the New York
    Herald Tribune called "a routine costume
    piece."

886. Stowe, Harriet Beecher. Uncle Tom's Cabin.
    Boston: John P. Jewett, 1852.

    The little book that started it all. Set
    in antebellum Kentucky.

887. Stowe, Rosetta. Cannons and Roses. New
      York: Dell, 1979.

      Three women on a Louisiana plantation
      react differently to the war. One becomes a
      Confederate spy. Another bears a slave's
      child and becomes an abolitionist. The
      third is non-political.

888. Straight, Michael W. A Very Small Remnant.
      New York: Knopf, 1963.

      Union soldiers massacre Cheyenne Indians
      at Sand Creek in 1864.

889. Stratemeyer, Edward. Defending His Flag.
      Boston: Lee & Shepard, 1907.

      The Battle of Manassas is the setting.

      Strebor, Eiggam. See Roberts, Maggie

890. Street, James Howell. By Valour and Arms.
      New York: Dial, 1944.

      A vivid, realistic portrait of the build-
      ing of a Confederate ship, the Arkansas,
      which destroyed part of Farragut's fleet in
      1862.

891. ————. Captain Little Axe. Philadelphia:
      Lippincott, 1956.

      A company of teenagers dies fighting for
      the South at Chicamauga.

892. ————. Tap Roots. New York: Dial, 1946.

      Explores the alleged secession of Jones
      County, Mississippi from the Confederacy.

893. Stribling, T.S. The Forge. New York:
      Doubleday, 1931.

      A middle-class Alabama family tries to
      endure the dislocations of war and its
      aftermath.

894.   ————. The Store. New York: Doubleday, 1932.

A novel about Confederate veterans and Klan members in the 1880s.

895.   Strohl, Paul. The Quarrel. New York: Duell, 1947.

896.   Swallow, James Francis. A Romance of the Siege of Vicksburg. Boston: Chapple, 1925.

897.   Swanberg, W.A. First Blood. New York: Scribner, 1957.

A Union major defends Fort Sumter despite being outnumbered.

898.   Tate, Allen. The Fathers. New York: Putnam, 1938.

Set in Virginia, this is "a beautifully written and profoundly searching story of the Old South," said The New York Times.

899.   Tatum, Edith. When the Bugle Called. New York: Neale, 1908.

A captain leaves his family to join his company in the Spring of 1861.

900.   Taylor, Walter E. The Night of the Dixie Wilds. Boston: Meador, 1929.

A novel of Reconstruction days by a man who was once a scout and guide for the Klan.

901.   Tenney, Sarah M. At Anchor. New York: Appleton, 1865.

A pro-Northern romance.

902.   Terhune, Albert Payson. Dad. New York: Watt, 1914.

A man dismissed from the U.S. Army during the Mexican War becomes a hero at Antietam.

903. [Terhune, Mary Virginia Hawes]. <u>Sunnybank</u>.
      New York: Sheldon, 1866.

      A romance which combines Union sentiments
      with respect for the South.

      Thane, Elswyth. See Beebe, E.T.

      Thanet, Octave. See French, Alice

904. Thomas, Theresa. <u>Tall Grey Gates</u>. New
      York: Ryerson, 1942.

      A Union soldier is captured and spends a
      horrible year in a Confederate prison in
      Salisbury, North Carolina.

905. Thomas, W.H. <u>Running the Blockade</u>. Boston:
      Lee & Shepard, 1875.

      Union spies fight blockade runners.

906. Thomason, John William. <u>Gone to Texas</u>. New
      York: Scribner, 1937.

      A Northern officer woos and wins a
      Southern woman after a Texas battle. The
      novel shows the difficult readjustment
      period in Texas after the war.

907. ————. <u>Lone Star Preacher</u>. New York:
      Scribner, 1941.

      The incredible military adventures of
      Praxiteles Swan, a Methodist preacher in the
      Army of Northern Virginia.

908. Thompson, Augustin. <u>A Waif in the Conflict
      of Two Civilizations</u>. Boston: Rapid
      Printing Company, 1892.

      A romance set in Tennessee.

909. Thomsen, Robert. <u>Carriage Trade</u>. New York:
      Simon & Schuster, 1972.

      An actor, a doctor and a dance hall
      hostess treat wounded soldiers in a saloon
      during the Battle of Gettysburg.

910. Thruston, Lucy Meacham. Called to the
     Field. Boston: Little, Brown, 1906.

     A newly-wed Virginia girl keeps the home
     fires burning.

911. Tiernan, Mary Spear. Jack Horner. New
     York: Fenno, 1890.

     A romance set in Richmond during the final
     year of the war.

912. Todd, Helen. A Man Named Grant. Boston:
     Houghton Mifflin, 1940.

     A biographical novel of a "failure."

913. Toepfer, Ray Grant. Scarlet Guidon. New
     York: Coward, 1958.

     Alabama soldiers fight at Gettysburg and
     in the Shenandoah.

914. ————. The Second Face of Valor.
     Philadelphia: Chilton, 1966.

     A young man enlists in the Confederate
     Army in Virginia and becomes a guerilla
     fighter in the Shenandoah.

915. Toepperwein, Herman. Rebel in Blue. New
     York: Morrow, 1963.

     A Union banker and spy poses as a
     Southerner in Texas.

916. Tomlinson, Everett Titsworth. For the Stars
     and Stripes. Boston: Lothrop, Lee &
     Shepard, 1909.

     A pro-Union story about escaping
     prisoners.

917. ————. The Young Blockaders. Boston:
     Lothrop, Lee & Shepard, 1910.

     For a change this story concentrates on
     the efforts of those who tried to maintain

the Union blockade, rather than the blockade runners.

918. ———. The Young Sharpshooters. Boston: Houghton Mifflin, 1913.

Two brothers enlist together in McClellan's Peninsula Campaign of 1862.

919. ———. The Young Sharpshooters at Antietam. Boston: Houghton Mifflin, 1914.

920. Tompkins, Jane. Cornelia. New York: Crowell, 1959.

The adventures of a Civil War nurse.

921. Tourgee, Albion Winegar. Bricks Without Straw. New York: Ford, 1880.

Two freed negroes and a Northern-born white female schoolteacher try to improve the lot of the black community in postwar North Carolina. The teacher also falls in love with and marries a former Confederate soldier.

922. ———. Figs and Thistles. New York: Ford, 1879.

923. ———. A Fool's Errand. New York: Ford, 1879.

A Union soldier moves his family to a North Carolina plantation after the war and socializes with Yankee schoolteachers from a black school. The Klan and other diehard Southerners make their life miserable.

924. ———. The Invisible Empire. New York: Ford, 1883.

A vivid account of Klan activities by the white South's severest critic.

925. ———. John Eax and Mamelon. New York: Ford, 1882.

The black sheep of an aristocratic North
Carolina family becomes a Union general.

926. ————. A Royal Gentleman and Zouri's
      Christmas. New York: Ford, 1881.

A white man takes a black mistress but
society prevents their marriage. In the
second story, kindly whites bring Christmas
to an orphaned black girl on a plantation in
1875.

927. ————. A Son of Old Harry. New York:
      Bonner, 1891.

928. ————. Toinette. New York: Ford, 1874.

An earlier version of A Royal Gentleman.

929. Townsend, George Alfred. Katy of Catoctin.
      New York: Appleton, 1886.

Called a "national romance," this
potboiler begins with John Brown's Raid and
ends with the conviction of the Booth
conspirators. Interwoven is a romance set
among German-Americans in the countryside of
western Maryland.

930. Tracy, Don. On the Midnight Tide. New
      York: Dial, 1957.

Two brothers from Wilmington, North
Carolina join the blockade runners.

931. Tracy, J. Perkins. The Blockade Runner.
      New York: Street and Smith, 1896.

A North Carolina boy supports the Union
though his uncle and guardian is a staunch
Confederate. The uncle forbids his adopted
daughter to see the young man even though
she loves him.

932. ————. Shenandoah. New York: Novelist
      Publishing Co., 1894.

Sheridan's Campaign.

933. Travers, Libbie Miller. The Honor of a
     Lee. New York: Cochrane, 1908.

     General Braxton Bragg campaigns in
     Tennessee.

934. Trowbridge, John Townsend. Cudjo's Cave.
     Boston: Tilton, 1864.

     A portrait of two daring black men. One,
     educated and sensitive, joins the Union
     Army. But the other kills his tormentors
     before dying himself.

935. ————. The Drummer Boy. Boston: Tilton,
     1863.

     A Union drummer boy acquits himself
     admirably at the Battle of Roanoke Island
     and also finds a long lost brother.

936. ————. The Three Scouts. Boston: Tilton,
     1865.

     A tale of Tennessee Unionists.

937. Tyler, C.W. The Scout. Nashville:
     Cumberland Press, 1911.

     A fictional portrait of the famed
     Confederate scout, Sam Davis.

938. Tyrrell, Henry. Shenandoah. New York:
     Putnam, 1912.

     Love and war in the valley.

939. Upchurch, Boyd. The Slave Stealer. New
     York: Weybright and Talley, 1968.

     An itinerant peddlar in the Southern
     mountains helps runaway slaves escape.

940. Vance, Wilson. God's War. New York: F.
     Tennyson Neely, 1899.

     A one-time British soldier fights for the
     South in Tennessee.

941. Van Loon, Antonia. <u>For Us the Living</u>. New
     York: St. Martin's, 1976.

     An upper middle class New York woman is in
     love with two men - one a wealthy officer
     and war hero and the other a disgruntled
     battlefield surgeon whom she meets on the
     fields of Gettysburg.

942. Van Praag, Francis W. <u>The Weaving of Webs</u>.
     New York: R.F. Fenno, 1902.

     A spy novel set in Richmond.

943. Van Zandt, Edmund. <u>The Seventh Girl</u>. New
     York: McGraw-Hill, 1970.

     A Confederate soldier from West Texas is
     disillusioned by the war.

944. Vaughn, Matthew. <u>Major Stepton's War</u>. New
     York: Doubleday, 1978.

     A Confederate officer escapes from a Union
     prison and leads a raid on a bullion depot
     in Massachusetts.

945. Venable, Clarke. <u>Mosby's Night Hawk</u>.
     Chicago: Reilly & Lee, 1931.

     A dashing adventure tale centered on
     Mosby's irregulars.

946. Verne, Jules. <u>Texar's Revenge</u>. Chicago:
     Rand McNally, 1888.

     A kind of spy novel set mostly in northern
     Florida.

947. Vidal, Gore. <u>Lincoln</u>. New York: Random
     House, 1984.

     A study of Lincoln's war years which
     readers seemed to like better than
     reviewers. <u>Time</u> said it was "just about all
     bad, including the prose."

948. Von Kreisler, Max. <u>Stand in the Sun</u>. New
     York: Doubleday, 1978.

A Union colonel is sent to the Plains in
late 1864 to stop a Confederate-inspired
Indian uprising.

949. Votaw, Clarence E. Patriotism.
      Philadelphia: Dorrance, 1941.

A Northern girl loves a Southern boy in
this strange novel.

950. Wagner, Constance. Ask My Brother. New
      York: Harper, 1958.

A Southern woman marries a Yankee and
settles in Pennsylvania during wartime.

951. Waldman, Emerson. Beckoning Ridge. New
      York: Henry Holt, 1940.

Bewilderment and despair grip a small
community of farmers in the western Virginia
hills as Confederate fortunes worsen.

952. Walker, Margaret. Jubilee. Boston:
      Houghton, Mifflin, 1966.

The daughter of a slave struggles to build
a better life for herself and her children.

953. Wallace, Willard M. The Raiders. Boston:
      Little, Brown, 1970.

A Union spy is nestled on a Confederate
ship.

954. Walworth, Mrs. Jeannette Haderman. On the
      Winning Side. New York: Collier, 1893.

Antebellum life in a Mississippi college
town.

955. Ward, Larry. Thy Brother's Blood. Los
      Angeles: Cowman, 1961.

A standard tale about two brothers who
chose opposite sides.

956. Warren, Joseph. The General. New York:
      Grosset & Dunlap, 1927.

A farce based roughly on the story of
Andrew's Raiders. This is the novel version
of a popular Buster Keaton silent movie.

957. Warren, Robert Penn. Band of Angels. New
York: Random House, 1955.

A white Kentucky girl discovers that her
mother had been a slave on the plantation.
She is sold and taken to New Orleans, where
she struggles to be free again. A former
lover reappears as a Union soldier.

958. ————. Wilderness. New York: Random
House, 1961.

A lame Bavarian Jewish poet comes to the
U.S. to fight for the Union in this
philosophical novel. He lands in New York
during the draft riots and finally reaches
Union lines as a civilian during the Battle
of the Wilderness.

959. Warren, Rose Harlow. A Southern Home in War
Times. New York: Broadway Publishing,
1914.

A series of vignettes that has no plot or
well-conceived plan.

960. Warwick, Bradfute. The Rock. New York:
Broadway Publishing, 1913.

Exploits of two Georgia soldiers in
northern Virginia.

961. Watson, Thomas Edward. Bethany. New York:
Appleton, 1904.

A young Confederate volunteer loves and
loses a Southern girl of rare promise and
beauty. Then he loses his life.

962. Watson, Virginia Cruse. The Featherlys.
New York: Dutton, 1936.

The saga of a distinguished Virginia
family.

Weaver, Ward. See Mason, Francis VanWyck

963. Webb, Christopher. Mark Toynman's Inheritance. New York: Funk & Wagnalls, 1960.

A fourteen-year-old boy and his aunt travel by wagon to California where he works in the Gold Rush. When the war begins he joins the Union Army and fights at Shiloh, Vicksburg and in the Wilderness Campaign.

964. Webber, Everett and Olga. Bound Girl. New York: Dutton, 1949.

Romance and bitter divisions coexist in the Kansas-Missouri border country. The New York Times said, "Most of the people behave exactly as though they were fugitives from a Burl Ives ballad."

965. Weber, William. Josh. New York: McGraw-Hill, 1969.

A humorous tale of a sixteen-year-old Southern boy who searches for his horse, which was stolen by Yankees.

966. Webster, Henry Kitchell. Traitor and Loyalist. New York: Macmillan, 1904.

The Union blockade of cotton shipments causes serious financial hardship to the South.

967. Weekley, Robert. The House in Ruins. New York: Random House, 1958.

A small band of rebels in Mississippi refuse to give up after Appomattox. They harass Union occupying troops. Library Journal called it a "dramatic story told with quiet dignity."

968. Wellman, Manly Wade. Appomattox Road. New York: Washburn, 1960.

Diehard Confederates fight on despite defeat.

969. ————. The Ghost Battalion. New York:
Washburn, 1958.

A young man joins the "Iron Scouts," a
brave Confederate group working behind Union
lines, but he's captured.

970. ————. Rebel Mail Runner. New York:
Holiday House, 1954.

The daring story of a boy who worked for
the Confederate underground mail service in
Pike County, Missouri. He was arrested but
pardoned by Lincoln.

971. ————. Ride Rebels. New York: Washburn,
1959.

The gallant exploits of the Confederate
Iron Scouts who ride with Jeb Stuart.
Second of the trilogy (The others are The
Ghost Batallion and Appomattox Road).

972. Wellman, Paul. Angel With Spurs.
Philadelphia: Lippincott, 1942.

A group of diehard Confederates go to
Mexico to begin life anew. They get
involved in the Mexican strife in this
action novel.

973. West, Jessamyn. The Friendly Persuasion.
New York, Harcourt, 1945.

Even gentle Quakers in Indiana are
disturbed by the war.

974. Westall, William. The Princes of Peele.
New York: Lovell, 1892.

The saga of Southern aristocrats, some of
whom marry and go to England.

975. [Weston, Mrs. Maria]. Bessie and Raymond.
Boston: Weston, 1866.

Two lovers are parted in this pro-Northern
romance.

976. Wheeler, A.O. Eye Witness. Boston:
     Russell, 1865.

     A cloak and dagger tale of the adventures
     of Southern Unionists.

977. Wheelwright, Jere Hungerford. Gentlemen,
     Hush! New York: Scribner, 1948.

     Deals mostly with Mosby's Rangers and
     Reconstruction days in Virginia.

978. ————. The Gray Captain. New York:
     Scribner, 1954.

     The second Maryland infantry fights
     valiantly and tragically for the Southern
     cause in a novel that the New York Herald
     Tribune said, "will bring tears to the eyes
     of Southerners."

979. Wheelwright, John T. War Children. New
     York: Dodd, Mead, 1908.

     The war as seen through the eyes of two
     Northern boys.

     White, Dale. See Place, Marian T.

980. White, Homer. The Norwich Cadets. St.
     Albans, VT: Albert Clarke, 1873.

     Students from Vermont's only military
     academy flock to the Union banners and fight
     in Virginia.

981. White, Leslie. Look Away, Look Away. New
     York: Random House, 1944.

     A fascinating story of the trek of
     Southerners to Brazil after the war. They
     find hardship but endure and vow never to
     return to the United States.

982. Whiting, John Downer. The Trail of Fire.
     Indianapolis: Bobbs Merrill, 1930.

     The story of the famous Confederate ship,
     Alabama.

983. Whitman, Sidney E. <u>Cavalry Raid</u>. Boston:
Houghton Mifflin, 1956.

The retelling of Colonel Benjamin
Grierson's sixteen-day foray into the South.
His fantastic feat is seen through the eyes
of a scout, a Southerner loyal to the Union
because of personal hatred.

984. Whitney, James H. <u>Father By Proxy</u>.
Hicksville, NY: Exposition Press, 1955.

Reconstruction days in Florida.

985. Whitney, Louise M. <u>Goldie's Inheritance</u>.
Burlington, VT: Free Press Association,
1903.

The siege of Atlanta.

986. Whitney, Phyllis. <u>The Quicksilver Pool</u>.
New York: Appleton, 1955.

A loveless marriage between a Union
soldier and a Southern girl, which takes
place on Staten Island.

987. ————. <u>Step To the Music</u>. New York:
Crowell, 1953.

A Staten Island family is divided by the
war, when the father joins the Union Army
and the daughter's boyfriend joins the
Rebels.

988. Whitson, Mrs. L.D. <u>Gilbert St. Maurice</u>.
Louisville: Bradley & Gilbert, 1875.

The heroism of the inhabitants of a
Tennessee town.

989. Whittlesey, Sarah J.C. <u>Bertha the Beauty</u>.
Philadelphia: Claxton, 1872.

An utterly ridiculous romance.

990. Wibberley, Leonard. <u>The Wound of Peter
Wayne</u>. New York: Farrar, 1955.

Moving from Reconstruction Georgia to Colorado, this story shows how a Southern veteran's bitterness is healed by his experiences in a Colorado gold field.

991. Wicker, Tom. <u>Unto This Hour</u>. New York: Viking, 1984.

A detailed novel about the Second Battle of Manassas. Actor Richard Harris called this "a dramatic, gory personal story, biblical in cadence and Tolstoyan in mood."

992. Willett, Edward. <u>True Blue</u>. New York: American News Company, 1865.

A novella about a wealthy North Carolina planter who is loyal to the Union. Though he is imprisoned and his family harassed and property confiscated, all ends well.

993. Williams, Ben Ames. <u>House Divided</u>. Boston: Houghton Mifflin, 1947.

A massive novel about Southern aristocrats who are related to Lincoln. Factual and absorbing.

994. ⸺⸺. <u>The Unconquered</u>. Boston: Houghton Mifflin, 1953.

Politics and romance in Reconstruction New Orleans.

995. Williams, Churchill. <u>The Captain</u>. Boston: Lothrop, 1903.

Grant as hero.

996. Williams, Dorothy Jeanne. <u>The Confederate Fiddle</u>. Englewood Cliffs: Prentice-Hall, 1962.

A young lad joins a wagon train to sell cotton and bring badly needed supplies to Confederate troops.

997. Williams, Flora McDonald. <u>The Blue Cockade</u>. New York: Neale, 1905.

War, fever and enthusiasm grip Virginia in this deeply pro-Southern tale.

998. ———. <u>Who's the Patriot?</u> Louisville: Courier-Journal, 1886.

A pro-Southern romance about a Charleston family.

999. Williams, George Forrester. <u>Bullet and Shell</u>. New York: Ford, 1883.

Exclusively military scenes.

Williams, J.R. See Williams, Dorothy

1000. Williams, John S. <u>The Siege</u>. New York: Cosmopolitan, 1912.

A Mississippi family survives the ordeal of the siege of Vicksburg.

1001. Willsie, Honore Morrow. <u>Benefits Forgot</u>. New York: Stokes, 1917.

The mother of a Union army surgeon, worried about her son's whereabouts, asks President Lincoln's help.

1002. Wilson, Annie E. <u>Webs of War in White and Black</u>. New York: Broadway Publishing, 1913.

Destruction and demoralization in Virginia late in the war.

1003. Wilson, Augusta Jane Evans. <u>Macaria</u>. New York: Bradburn, 1864.

Richard Harwell said this was "the literary sensation of the Confederacy and an all-time bestseller." The Union Army prohibited its being sold from within Union lines. It is a pro-Southern romance between a poor boy and a rich girl.

1004. Wilson, Charles Robert. <u>Bear Wallow Belles</u>. Louisville: R.J. Corothers, 1903.

A Union supporter knows his sweetheart is
a Rebel spy but he marries her anyway.

1005. Wilson, Dell B. The Grandfather and the
Globe. Bannner Elk, NC: Pudding Stone
Press, 1970.

Life in the Carolina Blue Ridge.

1006. Wilson, Kathrn Bemis. Blue Horses. Kansas
City, MO: Burton Publishing, 1931.

A biographical romance of a Union secret
service man.

1007. Wilson, Margaret. The Able McLaughlins.
New York: Harper, 1923.

A bitter, disillusioned farmer returns to
Iowa from Grant's army and discovers his
beloved is pregnant. He marries her and
tries to build a new life among the Scotch
immigrants.

1008. Wilson, William E. The Raiders. New York:
Rinehart, 1955.

An Ohio man saves a river town from a
party of marauding Rebels. He's a Democrat
whose son died a hero at Vicksburg.

1009. Winslow, Stanton. A Southern Girl. San
Francisco: Whitaker & Ray, 1903.

The romance of a young Congressman from
divided Indiana, who falls in love with a
Southern girl in Washington.

1010. Winslow, William Henry. Cruising and
Blockading. Pittsburgh: J.R. Weldin,
1885.

Florida's ports are blockaded.

1011. ————. Southern Buds and Sons of War.
Boston: C.M. Clark, 1907.

The upheavals of war disturb South
Carolina life.

1012. Winston, J. <u>Cora O'Kane</u>. Clarmont, NH:
      Privately Printed, 1868.

      A highly partisan pro-Union account of the
      "doom" of the Rebel guard in Missouri.

1013. Wise, John S. <u>The Lion's Skin</u>. New York:
      Doubleday, 1905.

      Reconstruction Virginia.

1014. Woerner, John Gabriel. <u>The Rebel's
      Daughter</u>. Boston: Little, Brown, 1899.

      A long, boring tale of love, politics and
      war.

1015. Wolford, Nelson. <u>The Southern Blade</u>. New
      York: Morrow, 1961.

      A Union captain relentlessly hunts down
      seven Confederates who escaped a P.O.W.
      camp.

1016. Wood, Benjamin. <u>Fort Lafayette</u>. New York:
      Carleton, 1862.

      A mildly pro-Southern novel written by a
      Democratic member of Congress from the
      North.

1017. Wood, Lydia Cope. <u>The Haydocks' Testimony</u>.
      Philadelphia: Christian Arbitration and
      Peace Society, 1890.

      Southern Quakers oppose war and slavery to
      the dismay of their neighbors.

1018. Woodiwiss, Kathleen E. <u>Ashes in the Wind</u>.
      New York: Avon, 1979.

      A New Orleans plantation-bred beauty falls
      hopelessly in love with the Yankee surgeon
      who rescues her.

1019. Woods, Mrs. Kate Tannatt. <u>Six Little
      Rebels</u>. Boston: Lothrop, 1879.

Six Southern youngsters survive the war in Washington, D.C.

1020. Wyman, Levi Parker. After Many Years. Philadelphia: Dorrance, 1941.

Concentrates on the plight of Quadroon women.

1021. Yerby, Frank. Captain Rebel. New York: Dial, 1956.

A New Orleans gambler fights the Union blockade by running arms and supplies from England.

1022. ———. Griffin's Way. New York: Dial, 1962.

A war veteran, master of a once great plantation, returns home to personal tragedy and romantic uncertainty. To top it all off the Klan comes to town.

1023. ———. McKenzie's Hundred. New York: Doubleday, 1985.

A wartime romance of two sisters who marry the wrong men. Publisher's Weekly called it "rambling and unfocused" and "long on military strategy, gunsmithing, engineering, and sex of the swooning sort, all served up in a thick Southern drawl."

1024. ———. The Vixens. New York: Dial, 1947.

A Southern aristocrat who fought for the Union returns home in 1866, reestablishes his ancestral estate and marries a beautiful woman. Kirkus said it "has lust, blood and enormous vitality."

1025. Yopp, William Isaac. A Dual Role. Dallas: John F. Worley, 1902.

A romance of a Tennessee Confederate regiment.

1026. Young, Rosamond McPherson. <u>The Spy With Two Hats</u>. New York: McKay, 1966.

A Pinkerton operative spies for the Union and engages in hair-raising adventures.

1027. Young, Stark. <u>So Red the Rose</u>. New York: Scribner, 1934.

A loving and gracious picture of the Old South. Ellen Glasgow called it "a glass through which one sees the Old South radiantly alive."

1028. Zara, Louis. <u>Rebel Run</u>. New York: Crown, 1951.

In 1862 Union soldiers try to cut communications between Atlanta and Chattanooga by seizing a train. Most were captured and executed. The <u>Chicago Tribune</u> said this fictional recreation of that event "has the ring of authenticity and is notably exciting."

Subject Index

Abolitionists 85, 145, 195, 616, 665, 876. See
  also Underground railroad.
Alabama 106, 129, 200, 271, 346, 355, 382, 515,
  609, 618, 779, 815, 837, 854, 865, 878, 893-94,
  913
Andersonville Prison 139, 140, 182, 212, 408, 535
Andrews Raid 65, 336, 781, 791, 956, 1028
Antietam, Battle of 46, 97, 217, 488, 555, 557,
  629, 696, 698, 788, 863, 902, 919
Appomattox 47, 256, 279, 387, 446, 968
Aquila, Battle of 29
Arizona 319, 339, 541, 716
Arkansas 27, 92, 132, 302, 308, 451, 523-24, 545,
  570, 618, 767, 774
Atlanta 255, 300, 303, 547, 682, 985. See also
  Sherman's March

Bahamas 325, 880
Beauregard, General Pierre 553
Belle Island Prison 536, 660
Benjamin, Judah P. 1, 178, 272
Bermuda 577, 661
Blacks 104, 115, 121, 175, 192, 195, 340, 348,
  382, 401, 403, 436-37, 466, 504, 515, 590, 593,
  662, 811, 836, 858, 878, 934, 952, 1020. See
  also Slaves, Underground Railroad
Blockade Running 10, 108, 203, 224, 322, 325,
  367, 456, 522, 577, 582, 595, 630, 661, 688,
  719, 880, 905, 917, 930-31, 966, 1010, 1021
Booth, John Wilkes 396, 526, 548, 869, 877
Boyd, Belle 188, 533, 713
Bragg, General Braxton 933
Brice's Crossroads, Battle of 388
Bull Run - see Manassas

California 91-2, 347, 447, 676, 963
Camp Followers - see Prostitutes
Canada 501, 772
Cape Cod 595

149

Title Index